JOHN JENNINGS 1965

1969

100 WATERCOLOR TECHNIQUES

Edited by Susan E. Meyer

100 WATERCOLOR TECHNIQUES

By Norman Kent N.A.,A.W.S.

Watson-Guptill Publications · New York

To my daughters: Mary and Suzanne
who enjoy watercolors

Contents

8

No PAINTING METHOD is more natural to the effervescent American temperament than watercolor, and it is for this reason that of all the national schools none has exploited the full range of this medium in recent time as successfully as the artists of our fifty states.

While the heavier and more thoroughly respected medium of oil on canvas held the affection of the painters from Colonial times through the nineteenth century, by the beginning of the second half of *this* century watercolor in the United States had become so popular with artists that it was in danger of becoming an art club fetish—like teacup reading or miniature golf.

But fortunately, as volume and competition increased, the light, clever effects of the facile renderers gave way before the more robust work of certain leaders, and individuality, that had all but disappeared through the methodology of summer school sessions, began to reassert itself in the examples by our most mature painters.

Artists like Winslow Homer, John Singer Sargent, Dodge McKnight, John Marin, Maurice Prendergast, Edward Hopper, and Charles Burchfield established unmistakable watercolor manners, but these were not the outgrowth of self-conscious style. Rather these were as natural and individual to each of them as their fashion of speaking or walking.

But strangely enough, though the present generation of artists has been brought up on the celebrity of these painters in watercolor, it was at most an indirect influence, for it had not been *their* lot or mission to make the medium popular as teachers of technique, since in every case, they were independent masters of their craft—and without exception, they were more solitary than most artists.

It is not easy therefore to assess the influences that have brought watercolor to the level of its present acceptance, especially among picture buyers and picture collectors. At a time when in so many instances painting in oil and polymer has sought gigantic scale—muralesque in size and outside the province of any but a museum or a castle to accommodate—the watercolor's average size (even when generously matted and framed) lends itself most agreeably to the limited walls of the small private home, and to the collector or museum; its ease of handling and storage is in its favor.

Another factor that has stimulated its production is that the color key of the average watercolor, being higher, brighter, and gayer than the average oil, makes it tasteful to relate to the general lively coloration and atmosphere of the contemporary home or apartment.

But for years, in spite of the uninterrupted annual exhibitions of the American Watercolor Society (founded in 1866)—proof that watercolor in America has achieved a whole century of practice and tradition—there was a hostile attitude on the part of the official art world (which in turn influenced the museum, the collector, and the professional easel painter) that the medium was an interloper—at best, only a sketch medium, too light in substance to be taken seriously, and being painted on paper, too fragile to last.

Though these inbred objections have not entirely disappeared—there are still home owners who yearn for a hand-painted oil to complement the luxury and status of a wood-burning fireplace—the idea that watercolors are too fragile to last has been dissipated by the persistent testimony that all-rag paper (on which most good watercolors are painted, like *all* the original prints and drawings of the Renaissance) will hold up for about as long in the future as man respects the artistic records of his past.

Since the general technique of painting in watercolor is so simple that it provokes no inhibitions in children, it is not strange that many older artists claim to have developed their own direction from a study of the work of their peers, as well as a concentrated period of trial and error.

The technical commentaries of the watercolorists in this book indicate again and again that though the basic tools are common, the different ways in which they are employed to obtain desirable effects point up the great variety of expression that exists—even in a medium, that more than any other, is loosely bound by a strong pictorial tradition.

And while no book or even a national exhibition can presume to contain every aspect of watercolor—every nuance of its myriad methods that are so sensitive to the artist's touch, so responsive to his temperament—the present compilation, representing the work of one hundred artists, certainly covers a wide area of these factors.

It should not be astonishing to anyone that the majority of watercolors here reflect the American landscape scene, for consistent with the strong background of its tradition—both oriental and occidental—the medium has been largely exploited for the expression of nature's moods found in her weather, in her light, and in her infinite variety. But scattered among the landscape paintings, the reader will find paintings dealing with other subject matter: the human figure, still life, and architecture.

And while pure, transparent color wash applied to the dry or dampened paper dominates the basic methods described, and revealed in the reproductions, there are also present fine examples of the admixture of opaque passages—casein, tempera, or gouache.

But binding all these facets together, and even putting aside the fact that the medium of watercolor is common to all, the reader is presented one hundred paintings that contain many demonstrations of sound design and expressive drawing—the two foundational disciplines that cannot be overstressed, and without which a picture—like "a house built on the sand"—falls apart.

Finally, the author wishes to express his indebtedness to the ninety-nine who, having contributed to the Watercolor Page of *American Artist* that formed the reservoir for their inclusion, generously consented to the excerpting of their technical testimony and the reproduction of their watercolors. And his thanks are also due to the editor, Susan Meyer, for her industry and patience; and to Donald Holden and Jules Perel for their consent to certain special conditions, his fraternal appreciation.

Norman Kent

Edward A. Anderson

Evening Express
Watercolor 17½" x 29"
Collection, William R. Harris

Edward a. anderson works almost exclusively in his studio. His paintings, by and large, result from remembered, nostalgic images related to the experiences and places that have personal meaning to him.

Anderson paints on 300 lb, medium or rough, top quality watercolor paper. He first soaks the sheet in the shower for about a half hour. While the paper is soaking, he chooses his brushes. He owns *several hundred* brushes: flat sables, round sables, Chinese writing brushes, even a wide variety of hardware store sable and bristle work brushes. For each new picture, he picks out five or six brushes that seem best suited to the problem, and places them on the drawing table, which is really a plain slab door supported by two drafting tables. Since he stands when he works, the table is adjusted at slightly less than waist height.

Anderson keeps a complete set of the best available tube watercolors in the studio. For his palette, he selects a group of eight or ten colors that relate to the picture he has in mind; for some pictures he introduces touches of colored inks or opaque white. Placing the wet watercolor sheet on several layers of newspapers spread over the drawing board—without fastening down the paper —he lays in the underlying structure or pattern with very bold, rich washes, using only two or three colors. Before the color can dry, he returns the paper to the shower and, using a 2" flat sable housepainter's brush, or a small hearth broom, Anderson washes out most of the color, thus achieving the first imagery as light tints over the paper. This process is repeated until the surface develops a color and pattern life of its own.

He now places the wet painting in a hinged studio mat and sets it over the fireplace. While the picture is drying, he sits across the room and contemplates the linear aspects of the problem. Next, he usually makes large exploratory drawing studies, taking clues and suggested shapes from the wet painting, drawing on a large tablet in ink, charcoal, or soft pencil. This reversal of the general "drawing-before-painting" procedure keeps the imagery more flexible as the picture develops. When the painting is dry, he establishes the major linear elements in diluted black India ink, drawing over the washes with a ruling pen —held like a brush—a pipe cleaner, or a small branch from one of the trees outside the studio, depending on the line quality desired.

In most cases, the painting has now been in process for at least one day, sometimes longer. Because both sides of the paper are equally wet during the development of the painting, he has no serious buckling or twisting problems during its drying period. A good sheet of all-rag watercolor paper will take an astonishing amount of punishment. Finally, Anderson temporarily mats the picture and studies the results of his efforts.

Edward A. Anderson 13

14   Harry Anderson

Hᴀʀʀʏ ᴀɴᴅᴇʀsᴏɴ always works with tempera, a prepared, opaque tube color, using only those colors advertised by their makers as absolutely permanent, namely: burnt sienna, burnt umber, raw umber, yellow ochre, cadmium yellow, lemon yellow, permanent green light, permanent green deep, pogany blue (near cerulean), cobalt blue, ultramarine blue, alizarin crimson, vermilion, show-card white. He uses no violets or black. For his darks, he combines pogany blue with alizarin or permanent green deep with alizarin.

He prefers a rough handmade watercolor paper, mounted on board in the heavy weights. His brushes are the finest grade red sables and oil bristle brushes, which he uses to paint any solid, opaque passages.

In painting a landscape—the picture reproduced here is his first portrait in watercolor—Anderson works directly from nature or from color slides. He makes no preliminary sketch, but works directly on the full sheet with brush and color. He has, however, a clear idea of the final composition by the time he puts brush to paper.

As he starts to paint, he lays in all the color areas as quickly as possible so that the arrangement becomes clear. He pays little attention to detail at this stage. Starting with the sky and the distance, Anderson works toward the foreground. He pays particular attention to the sky in his painting, believing that the sky should be a foil for the rest of the design.

When dry, his tempera color has almost the same appearance as transparent color. (For that matter, most colors found in any "transparent" palette are not really transparent, but appear so only because of their dilution with water.) Sometimes Anderson applies solid opaques in finishing paintings. To lighten or change a passage, he hesitates to use solid, opaque color, and apply light on dark. He prefers to scrub out the area first and then repaint it.

Frequently, the artist uses his fingers or, more accurately, his thumbs in manipulating the color for different effects. He is always watchful for desirable "accidental" passages which, when found effective, he is careful to retain.

Anderson uses two different colors on a single bristle brush when he paints objects whose color might run from light to dark—such as a cylinder, for example. First he loads the brush with the lighter hue and then, with a section of the brush, he picks up the darker paint so that when the stroke is made, very interesting accidental effects result. This works very well on small objects.

At times he carries his partly finished outdoor paintings to the studio for completion. After he has tentatively finished a painting, he turns its face against a wall for several days and then brings it out for a fresh look. He may examine it upside down or in a mirror to detect any flaws. Following this, final corrections are made and the painting is ready for framing.

16　Tore Asplund

Tore asplund generally paints his watercolors from his oil sketches. Very often these sketches are made from inside an auto, which permits him to work in tough weather—rain, snow, or cold—often the ideal time for an engaging atmosphere. He uses a 12" x 16" paint box which he can hold in his lap, and paints on canvas held in its cover. He finds this combination quite comfortable, even in a small car. When he is able to work outside, Asplund has a photographer's aluminum tripod which he can fasten to a flange riveted to the bottom of the box. At times when he is in a foreign country where luggage is apt to be a burden, he may use a 9" x 12" or even a smaller sketch box.

For his oil sketches, Asplund uses a rather limited palette which consists of the following oil colors: white, cadmium yellow pale, cadmium yellow medium, cadmium orange, cadmium red, burnt sienna, cobalt blue, ultramarine blue, viridian, black, and turpentine for his medium. He uses a fairly smooth linen canvas, and uses his paint quite thin. This helps him to work faster. At times Asplund has a damp-stretched full sheet of cold pressed paper, which he coats with gum arabic while it is still wet. When it is dry and flat, he cuts it to the size he wishes to use. This make a fine white surface to work on in oils, and he believes it is quite permanent.

For his oil sketches, Asplund uses four or five flat sable brushes, two or three flat bristle brushes, and a few watercolor brushes. He also finds a striper—a brush with long thin hair, almost like a pencil lead—very useful. These can be made by trimming the hair from an old large watercolor brush, leaving only enough of the center hair to make a thin line. This can be used like a pen for drawing architectural ornaments, tree branches, and other similar details.

Asplund finds it better not to be too particular in searching for a subject; he paints at the first likely spot. Something may not look too good at first, but may turn out to be better than expected. Also, looking for something better further on, he might end up with nothing. Very often, if he finds *one* good subject in a certain locale there will be a number of other subjects that are suitable. He feels very happy if he manages one good sketch out of five.

For painting his watercolors in the studio, Asplund uses a Formica top paint table, about 20" x 30" in size. His palette is quite a bit larger than the one he uses for oil. He keeps his colors in small cups in a box, so that he can wash the cups out separately. These colors are cadmium yellow pale, cadmium yellow medium, cadmium yellow deep, cadmium orange, cadmium red, alizarin crimson, burnt sienna, burnt umber, phthalocyanine violet, cobalt blue, ultramarine blue, Payne's gray, phthalocyanine green, Hooker's green, and black.

Asplund uses the best sable watercolor brushes in sizes 4, 6, and 8; for larger brushes, he uses ones made of coarser hair and these are, of course, less expensive. He also uses a few bristle brushes, a soft sponge, and a very sharp knife.

Ralph Avery

Powers Tower
Watercolor 12" x 16"
Collection, Nicholas Agnello

Rᴀʟᴘʜ ᴀᴠᴇʀʏ refers to this small watercolor as a neighborhood sketch. It was composed of a group of old commercial buildings standing around the corner from his studio. He had seen it innumerable times in different lights, during day and night, and in a variety of weather conditions. In other words, the subject was in his mind and memory for some time before he attempted to paint it. He had, however, made two small, very rough sketches on the spot.

Powers Tower, like so much of Avery's work, was painted *primarily* from memory. He often prefers to work away from his subject, finding that the result is less cluttered by the detail and unimportant features that often creep in. He believes that the abstract patterns are what make or break a painting, not how accurately the work presents the illusion of reality. Therefore, when Avery paints a building, he is not concerned whether his building looks just like the one in front of him—it may be just a vague mass with little dots for windows. As long as that mass seems to be the right size, color, and shape, and is correctly placed, he is satisfied. In the case of *Powers Tower*, Avery's interest was initially sparked by the big splashes of color furnished by the billboards, butting against the long vertical dark mass of the building at the right, and the violent perspective of the middle distance buildings, making an unusual shape in the center. The automobiles, resembling small pieces of colored paper rushing along the damp reflecting streets, also caught his eye. They helped to give a feeling of scale.

Almost every imaginable technique was used in this 12" x 16" painting. It began as a transparent watercolor on a piece of novelty mat board (whose texture he likes for making trial sketches only, never for permanent painting). Regular watercolor brushes, sponges, rollers, and a carbon pencil for delicate lines and accents, each played a part. Towards the end, Avery even added a touch of opaque color where texture and solidity were needed—an effect not easily produced by a transparent wash. He finds that such small areas of color, when judiciously used, complement the transparent washes, making an attractive result.

20　Merrill A. Bailey

Since Merrill Bailey lives in central New York State, where the winters are rugged, he has become expert at painting in freezing temperatures. He does the greater portion of his outdoor winter sketching from a car. The necessity for comfort and convenience caused him to experiment with a simple folding gadget which fits on the back seat. It is a sheet of heavy plywood, with a folding leg which supports the end not resting on the seat. Measuring approximately 18″ x 36″, it has a hole in the top large enough to hold a two-quart pail of water. On this surface, which is level, there is ample room for his paper, a white enamel palette, cleansing tissues, and a folded turkish towel on which he lays his brushes. This platform leaves the arms and legs free to move.

He also uses an old-fashioned soapstone—the kind that was once used in the bottom of the sleigh. When this is thoroughly heated, wrapped in several layers of newspaper, and sat upon, it will keep one's rear end comfortable for several hours! Though the hands and feet will still suffer, he has found that he does some of his keenest thinking, grasping the essentials more quickly, with less tendency to overwork detail, than in the comfort of his studio. Sometimes, though seldom, these sketches become finished pictures without further work.

First Bailey sketches the basic composition lightly in pencil, then he blocks in the major elements. He first starts to paint the sky—the source of illumination— either wet or dry, avoiding hard edges. As soon after this as possible, he paints in one of the darkest darks, thus establishing the value key for the balance of the picture. This makes it easier to determine middle distance color values in correct relationships. By keeping the whole watercolor in a fluid state of development, he is able to take advantage of unexpected forms that occur in the washes and accents—patterns that can be integrated effectively.

Bailey uses three sable brushes: nos. 14, 10, and 6; and two flat-edged lacquer brushes—one ¾″ and one 2″. The latter two are used for wetting large areas quickly and also for laying subtle washes. His palette contains Winsor green, Winsor blue, cobalt blue, cadmium lemon, cadmium yellow medium and light, cadmium orange, cadmium red medium and light, alizarin crimson, burnt sienna, burnt umber, yellow ochre, Payne's gray, and ivory black. He never uses an easel; he prefers to work flat, tilting the board to control the washes.

Bailey uses a rough paper, in both the 140 and 300 lb weights. The lighter paper is dampened and stretched to dry flat on a drawing board; the heavier stock is taped down dry on all four sides. He also uses a pad of half sheet paper in the 140 lb weight, since he finds this size the most convenient one for working in the field. As a matter of fact, he paints and exhibits more half sheets than larger ones, and he firmly believes that too many large scale watercolors lack the quality more often obtained in the more moderate size.

Warren Baumgartner

Peggy's Cove, Nova Scotia
Watercolor 22" x 30"

Warren baumgartner (1894–1963) spent a large part of his professional life as a successful illustrator for national magazines. Once having discovered that watercolor was a natural medium for him, he often took time off from his commissioned work to paint independent pictures, and frequently traveled great distances to seek out motifs that, by hearsay, had captured his imagination.

Since the demands of illustration are based primarily on clear pictorial expression, good drawing, and control of the medium in which they are executed, it is not astonishing that artists trained and experienced in this profession often bring a compositional advantage to their easel pictures in watercolor. Such was true in Baumgartner's case. For example, study *Peggy's Cove*, reproduced on the facing page. First, note its strong design, built on a series of compelling movements that carry the eye to the right into the middle plane; then a strong counter-oblique from the right end of the long fence is picked up in similar angular accents in the clouds; and finally, the eye path is forced downward vertically from the top left area by another series of shorter passages of contrasting values, to the place of the beginning.

Baumgartner was happiest when doing an on-the-spot painting, whether for an exhibition picture or an editorial assignment. He believed that the illustrator should experiment with many media until he finds one that is especially responsive to his temperament and to his particular form of expression.

One of the special marks of Baumgartner's watercolors is that the beholder is not immediately conscious of the medium; the pictorial content comes through first. One reason that his pictures wear so well is that he was never satisfied with flashy effects—obviously textured passages, vagaries of form, or jarring notes of unrelated color.

Baumgartner used 300 lb paper, a paper heavy enough to take rather rough treatment—scraping with a razor blade and scrubbing with a sponge. His easel was French made—the tripod legs, hinged to the bottom of the box, unfolded and adjusted to any desired height. He used a drawer in the easel for his tubes of color and palette, and the paper was held by supports at any angle.

He considered his camera an important part of his traveling equipment. This enabled the artist to bring home every conceivable bit of pictorial information that he could use in illustration. And of course Baumgartner photographed everything along the way that might have been useful in future pictures.

24 C. C. Beall

C. c. beall uses a comfortable-sized white enamel tray on which he puts freshly squeezed colors. His palette is organized, from left to right, in this way: black, Payne's gray, phthalocyanine blue, Prussian blue, ultramarine blue, cerulean blue, emerald green, sap green, Hooker's green dark, raw sienna, Indian yellow, lemon yellow, orange, light red, carmine lake, rose madder, brown madder, and Van Dyke brown. He keeps a few jars of poster colors of the more brilliant hues handy and a large jar of poster white.

He buys only good sable brushes—those that will point well and hold their weight when saturated—the smallest, a no. 3, and four larger brushes up to a 2" wide flat brush.

Beall painted the abstract for the portrait of his daughter—the painting reproduced here—without wearing his glasses. After the pattern, color, and values seemed workable, he put on his glasses and had his daughter sit again so that he could add the essential drawing to obtain a likeness. He tried to keep the details from spoiling the big design. This portrait is the result of a good deal of experimentation. The painting was completed in watercolor on mounted paper. Then he took tracing paper, rolled it into a ball, saturated it with casein glue, and rolled it flat on the surface of the initial painting. When dry, the glue-sized paper gave him a fine top surface for the accents he needed.

This kind of experimentation is familiar to Beall. He was never satisfied painting watercolor in the traditional manner. Having been brought up artistically in the days when most illustration was done in monochrome wash—and having mastered it in his illustration—his facility was such that there was little challenge in going from a familiar brush technique with a single color to another that permitted the freedom of a full-color palette. Early in his career as a watercolorist, he explored various combinations of paper, wood, and paint. At first, he turned to the paper element, and after trying various surfaces of both watercolor and drawing papers, he decided that none quite suited him. So he began overlaying illustration board with tissue paper held down with a glue size. This resulted in a number of unusual textures successfully exploited in various portrait studies.

Next Beall turned to wood panels, and after coating these with a thin gesso ground, he used transparent watercolor to paint a number of special pictures in which the wood again was exploited in the movement of figures—even in the expression in some of his portraits.

26 Walter Biggs

WHEN AN ARTIST who has been much loved dies, it is natural for his friends to exaggerate his contributions to the arts, but in the case of Walter Biggs (1886-1968), it would be difficult. For not only was this fine artist recognized as one of the few deans of American illustration—his work in this field had graced periodicals, especially *Ladies' Home Journal*, for over forty years—but his stature as a watercolorist was never questioned by seasoned artists who knew his work, by all curators and museum directors who recognized quality when they saw it, and by a small coterie of discerning collectors who completely absorbed his intermittent production.

It is something of a paradox that Walter Biggs, who was trained as a painter, should have become so very successful as an illustrator—whose illustrations were more often mood pictures than literal interpretations of the text, and thereby prized as independent easel pictures (which they were not)—and that his truly separate paintings, both in oil and watercolor, showed no trace of a slick illustrational technique.

We can only conclude that this was true because Biggs never made a distinction between his commercial career as an illustrator and his parallel life as a painter. He brought the same integrity as a dedicated artist to every picture he painted—whether it was for reproduction in a magazine or a personal expression that might have longer life as an independent testament.

The present watercolor is a case in point. Though it was painted years ago in the small town in Virginia he knew and loved so well—and where he lived during the last years of his life—it is wholly characteristic of his impressionistic manner of expression. The brushwork is unself-conscious—one can only follow its pathway by dint of careful study; yet it has magic—creating firm forms in the foreground which in the back stretches of the street merge and blur to a satisfying indistinctness.

No camera has been used here (Biggs never used photography); only the eyes of a sensitive observer, steeped in familiar subject matter and in love with its every aspect.

How masterful every inch of this seemingly rapidly executed painting has been subtly adjusted to form a piture—a picture which in no way is dependent on the rendering of a particular place, but is *a work of art first*, and only secondarily, a watercolor.

28　David Blower

Tin Can Beach
Watercolor 14½″ x 22″
Collection, Phyllis Fedderson

For DAVID BLOWER, painting a watercolor directly from nature is a most exhilarating adventure, and it is a practice that he has assiduously followed for many years. He feels a first-rate watercolor painting is accomplished by the artist's adeptness in resolving the immediate problems of design and color, his skillful use of equipment, and by feeling out the painting with a preliminary rough sketch.

Blower finds the mood of the day an important consideration in his painting, and he usually waits for the later afternoon hours to ensure dramatic lighting. The prevailing weather sometimes has a good deal to do with the successful execution of a watercolor. During the fall and winter months in California, the air is so laden with moisture that it interferes with the drying time of large washes, and slows down the creative process. Nor is a hot summer's day desirable, when the problem can be just the opposite; the warm, thirsty paper can nullify the best intentions of a wet wash.

Blower's painting equipment is of his own assemblage: an old photographer's tripod, on which he has installed a motion picture camera tilt-top, connected to the back of a 20″ x 26″ x ⅜″ basswood drawing board. On the horizontal bottom of this board, he has glued a narrow strip of wood. This becomes the "holding" board and is attached, by threading, to the tripod in the same manner as a camera. On another basswood board, he tapes a half sheet of 300 lb watercolor paper. This board is placed directly upon the "holding" board, the ⅜″ strip preventing it from falling off when the board is in a tilted position. The artist may also turn the unattached board upside down for the manipulation of washes. The "holding" board is slightly thinner than the one that carries the paper. Blower has painted spar varnish on all of his equipment, since a good deal of water is splashed over it from time to time.

David Blower has six of the 20″ x 26″ basswood boards and three of the 23″ x 31″ size—the latter accommodating the full sheet. Occasionally, he uses the full sheet "in the field," but he has found it more expedient to use the half sheet.

His watercolor painting kit is also made up of various items, all born of necessity and experience. Into a compartmentalized (9¼″ x 12⅛″) aluminum oil box, he has glued fourteen porcelain paint saucers. The box is deep enough to take another strip of the same size with additional saucers; this fits right over the lower strip, but is placed on the lid when the box is opened for use. A supplementary white plastic palette fits alongside this second strip of colors, and when they are all spread out ready for painting, he has a range of thirty-eight colors. These are separated into three sections: the cools, the warms, and the earth colors. He never uses white. His brushes include a 2″ camel's hair brush for large washes; a Whitney dual; a 1″ flat sable; a 1″ horsehair; two ½″ ox hair; and several round sables ranging from no. 1 through no. 12. A folding stool, two half gallon water jars, tissues, and rags, complete his painting paraphernalia.

Betty M. Bowes

Pallas Athena
Watercolor 27" x 21"

Betty bowes uses a fairly simple palette, which is far from static, and the best materials available. Heavy, rugged, handmade papers are always her first choice, and the best sable brushes. She also employs a variety of implements, such as an ordinary putty knife (safely used on heavy paper), wooden sticks, a shaving brush for large washes, and razor blades to pull out sharp white areas while the color is still wet. She finds use for bits of mat board to lay opaque casein over transparent color, much in the manner of block printing. This procedure is highly satisfactory in adding textures to buildings, boats, and many other objects. It also causes interesting things to happen when an opaque color is laid partially over a transparent one. Sometimes, in the excitement of nearing completion, almost anything handy in the studio will get into the last few minutes of painting.

When she paints on location, the artist does *only* small sketches. All large paintings are done later in her studio with the help of these sketches, plus color photographs taken by her husband (although she is careful never to allow the photograph to impose itself too much upon the painting), plus a wide area of imagination which develops after time and space have elapsed between her vision and her experience.

Her approach to her painting varies with every object she paints, her procedure adapting itself to the subject, mood, and background of each new experience. A river scene, for instance, with all its ambient color, will be treated in an entirely different way from Greece where there is absolutely no ambience at all. Before she begins, the artist has a general idea of what she wants to put down on the paper. She sees it first with a kind of inner eye, then begins to paint directly, never drawing in first with pencil, since she finds it too confining. Her painting seldom comes out exactly as planned, but usually somewhere near, for she keeps at it until she approaches the mood she originally sought. A heavy, 300 lb paper that still holds its surface and flatness, can be completely sponged out for a new beginning if the painting should turn in an undesirable direction.

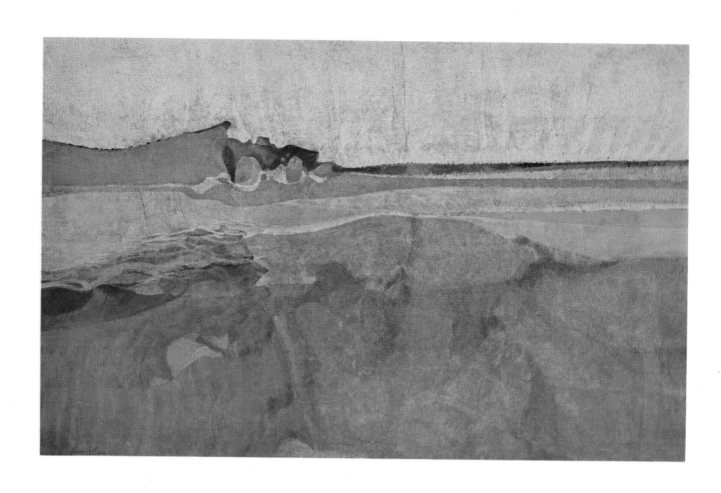

32   Glenn R. Bradshaw

GLENN BRADSHAW uses rather unusual materials. For paper, he prefers white Sekishu rice paper. He usually works on the full sheet size, about 25" x 39", and paints with casein that has been thinned to a liquid state. His brushes are ox hair lettering brushes up to 2" in width; various round watercolor brushes, including some of the Japanese variety; and ordinary housepaint brushes. He uses the lettering brushes for painting the large passages and reserves the conventional watercolor brushes for small areas. A large, round ox hair brush, which has been trimmed until only a flexible center tuft of hair remains, is his favorite tool for brush drawing and for linear elements in the paintings.

Bradshaw's palette is extensive and he regards the following colors as the minimum that he must have available: alizarin crimson, cadmium red light, cadmium red deep, cadmium orange, cadmium yellow pale, cadmium yellow deep, Naples yellow, raw sienna, burnt sienna, ultramarine blue, cobalt blue, phthalocyanine blue, phthalocyanine green, viridian, permanent green light, raw umber, burnt umber, terra rosa, ivory black, lamp black, and white.

All of Bradshaw's work is done in the studio. First he places his paper flat on a sheet of hardboard. Then, using the large lettering brushes and liquid paint, he develops—in less than five minutes—a bold non-objective composition in color. He does not refine any of the relationships at this stage.

He waits until one layer is dry before he proceeds with the next. Keeping a number of paintings in progress at the same time, he turns from one to another as drying permits. He paints several thin layers of color on *each side* of the paper; the paint penetrates so that washes intermix visually through the paper.

After applying three or four layers of paint, Bradshaw decides which side of the paper will be the front and which images he will develop. After making these decisions, he develops the painting further by applying additional color washes and brush lines. Sometimes dark colors are placed over light ones; at other times, light over dark. Some washes give an even veiling of color; others are mottled by blotting or brush strokes. He frequently uses washes of white, and often develops forms by painting the areas around them.

Mounting the painting is a delicate process. First the rice paper is placed face down on a large sheet of glass. Then the back is coated with wheat paste spread evenly with a 4" housepainter's brush. At this point, the paste-soaked paper is extremely fragile, so completing the mounting is a two-man job. The painting is picked up and turned over onto the illustration board and is rolled with a rubber brayer, which presses the paper and helps to remove air pockets and excess paste. Care is exercised to keep paste off the face of the painting and to smooth the paper without tearing it. As the paste dries, it may cause the illustration board to curl slightly. However, painting the back of the board with casein or diluted paste will offset this and restore the board's flatness. The mounted painting is usually trimmed flush and framed with a liner, rather than a mat.

Heidi Brandt

The Cala, Deya, Mallorca
Casein 8¾" x 15"

HEIDI BRANDT'S WORK is characterized by her ability to translate the significance of an arrested moment into visual expression with an exceptionally clear line or stroke. She practices and sketches whenever there is an opportunity to do so, searching always to catch a fleeting moment's duration, to record the transitory.

Her colors frequently are muted, but often contain strong contrasts. She does most of her paintings in casein (which lends itself to fast work and experimentation), applied with a sharp edged, flexible knife angled to a fine point. In almost all her paintings, she uses the knife for laying in the larger color areas and frequently for applying a ground tone of the predominating color. For details, the artist employs a brush in a dry and linear manner. Other fine points are brought out by using the point of the knife to scratch through to an underlying color. This is often done while she is painting in the larger color areas.

Her paintings begin on sketchbook paper in small format. Sometimes these sketches are no more than line drawings, with written notes. At other times they are in color with all the detail of a finished painting. If she then makes a larger painting, she works on Masonite surfaced with a gesso ground. To be satisfied with the finished work, she feels it must have the same intensity and freshness of feeling she achieved in her sketch.

The artist's sketch materials are always with her, whether she uses a scrap of paper, or the back of a program, or a menu at a café. At a concert, she may even sketch on her program in the dark. She fully realizes the ephemeral mood and moment; and that we never look at the same thing twice in exactly the same way.

36 Carl Broemel

Fishermen's Quarters, Ischia
Watercolor 16" x 28¼"

IN HIS WATERCOLOR TECHNIQUE, Carl Broemel prefers a loose handling which allows the wet colors to do some of the work, an approach he feels produces better results than a labored and overworked one. As a rule, he starts with the lightest areas, working from the top to the bottom in one "go." For him, watercolor is a snapshot medium. There is no time for mulling over the approach and little chance to make changes.

When he paints, Broemel has everything he needs at hand. He uses only the best quality equipment; a poor brush or the lack of one color—even if he doesn't need it—irritates him. He never knows what colors he may need, and he feels that a full display stimulates him. His brushes are of the finest red sable. His easel is light but sturdy. It can be tilted at any angle, adjusts to any ground surface, and folds into a simple, compact kit. He purchased it many years ago and it is still as good as ever. Broemel uses a standard metal watercolor box with twenty-four whole pans. In it he carries his generous supply of tube colors.

Since most papers are now mold-made and have too regular a surface for his liking, Broemel has found one made in England that is pasteless, all linen, and completely handmade. The heavy weight needs no mounting and one can paint on both sides, which is an economy.

Weather and seasons call for special consideration. At times Broemel uses an umbrella. While painting in the desert, he had to rig up a windbreak with an old blanket anchored by rope. He likes the stimulation of outdoor painting. Although he feels that studio work has its merits too—especially if one is trying for something more subjective—he finds a definite flavor to a sketch made outdoors.

Arnold Burchess

The Smokestack
Watercolor 17½" x 23¾"
Collection, Dr. L. Aledort

Arnold burchess believes that constant sketching is of vital necessity for a practicing artist as a means of visual rejuvenation and as a source of material for his more serious work. Sketching is a continuous pleasure for this artist. He is usually outdoors most weekends of the year—especially in the summer when he travels and sketches even more. He usually paints his sketches very directly, working on a 140 lb watercolor block approximately half the size of the standard 22″ x 30″ sheets.

Before he starts, Burchess visualizes what he wants, with special emphasis on a strong, dynamic composition in color, pattern, and dark and light. He finds the flat sable brushes very practical, inasmuch as he prefers hard urban and industrial scenes. (*The Smokestack*, reproduced here, is the result of a sketch made in Long Island City, New York.) The sketches are done quite rapidly, usually requiring about an hour to complete. He is never particularly happy about any sketch when he finishes it, but he has found that most of them constitute a sort of textbook of impressions when he peruses them after a period of time. In the winter, his sketches are models of brevity, when frozen fingers, holding the brush in a paralytic grip, force him to work in rapid motion.

These sketches form the basis for most of Burchess' serious work. Taking a detail from one, and a detail from another, he makes a few small preparatory drawings in watercolor, always keeping a good visual image of what the finished picture will be. The paper is almost always 140 or 300 lb cold pressed, although there have been times when only a hot pressed surface would do. His brushes are red sable, both pointed and flat. The colors used are nominal in quantity and range (he has not yet found a suitable red!).

Painting is a slow process for Burchess. He vacillates, ponders, and mulls it over—and then finally finds himself at that one moment of courage, face-to-face with the white paper, brush in hand. Finally, he applies the first wash and waits for it to dry. Then in succession, he lays in wash on wash.

40   Charles Burchfield

CHARLES BURCHFIELD (1893-1967) worked primarily from subjects found within a stone's throw of his home. He was always discovering something new in old, familiar things. Sometimes he would brood over a picture for a long time before his conception was finally realized; at other times, he would go out with his sketching kit and return in a few hours with a completed painting. But most of his pictures were carefully studied, and he would generally make a great many pencil drawings on location, familiarizing himself with details and color.

He may or may not have referred to these drawings when he finally began his painting, but through them he absorbed both the factual and emotional content of the scene. They were not so much sketches as diagrammatic data with written notes of colors and effects. Even in his final pencil composition—often squared up for transfer—the forms were indicated rather than meticulously defined; he left as much as possible for his brushes to do.

Before painting, Burchfield generally stretched his paper, regardless of its weight. First he wet the paper on both sides with a sponge; then he applied library paste with a 3″ varnish brush. Finally, he smoothed down the sheet on a piece of ⅛″ cardboard. To prevent warping, another sheet of ordinary wrapping paper was moistened and pasted to the reverse side of the cardboard. The mount was then put in a press to dry.

When he painted an exceptionally large watercolor—say 34″ x 54″—Burchfield would enlarge a 24″ x 36″ sheet of paper. He would add strips all around the edge, mounting all on a heavy piece of cardboard. To do this, he cut the edges with a razor blade along a metal straightedge. When carefully cemented to the board, with edges butted together, the seam was scarcely noticeable.

Burchfield used the following brushes: a red sable pointed brush, which he used rather infrequently in the conventional manner; three straight black sable brights—for all manner of painting; four brights, which were trimmed diagonally, used for drawing and painting; two pig-bristle brights cut off short, used for scrubbing out unwanted details. His practice of trimming his brushes diagonally was suggested by the manner in which they naturally wore down as he painted.

To paint a watercolor was as natural to Charles Burchfield as using a pencil, whereas he felt self-conscious when he used oil. In comparing oil to watercolor, Burchfield said, "To me watercolor is so much more pliable and quick. For instance, you decide that a whole passage is undesirable; you take a sponge and wipe it out in a few seconds. To do the same thing in oil is more complicated and takes more time."

Jack Burton

Amy
Watercolor 30" x 22"

Jack burton holds down his technique to a secondary position so that the pictorial content of the painting is not overshadowed by clever brushwork. To him, minimizing technique is one of the very important steps to a good watercolor.

Burton usually avoids painting on paper, because of the inconvenience of stretching or mounting, plus the necessity of transporting a drawing board on location. He prefers to use hot pressed *board* or the equally fine surface of cold pressed board. In the studio, the ready-mounted board is easier to move from drawing table or easel to picture frame, and stands less chance of damage.

In choosing a palette, Burton has found that a combination of transparent colors and gouache gives him a much greater range of expression than the use of transparent colors alone. On some occasions, he likes to use a semi-opaque gouache tone applied over a more brilliant transparent wash. This produces a vibrant depth not obtainable with the so-called "purest methods." The range of colors in his transparent paints is what he believes to be the usual selection for watercolorists, avoiding, however, dangerous colors such as Prussian blue, indigo, and chrome green. He also includes black in his palette. The opaque colors that he uses in conjunction with the transparent ones are much more limited: white; nos. 2, 3, and 4 grays; azure and ultramarine blue; violet and geranium lake pale are about all that he finds necessary.

Burton uses a rather unorthodox mixture of flat and round sable brushes. For paper soaking, he employs a 2" bristle brush or a common shaving brush. Working into damp surfaces gives him satisfactory results if great care is taken to time the application of paint to the wet surface. It is at this particular stage that he thinks the artist can get "carried away" with tricky puddled effects. At this point *he* exercises restraint. Having done this, smaller areas are then put in and the final stages of the picture completed.

In *Amy*, reproduced here, the pattern of the model's figure with the blue drape intrigued the artist. The relationship of these forms to the background seemed much more important than the literal forms of the remaining objects in the room. The color, therefore, was not realistically reported except where needed—in terms of design—on the figure and especially on the blue cloth.

Auburn Street Crossing
Watercolor 14″ x 21″

To OBTAIN A THIN UNDERPAINTING, Ranulph Bye has found success with a mixed media technique combining watercolor and thin washes of oil and turpentine laid in on wet paper. This approach works well for achieving wood, granular, or foliage effects and hence for anything needing an aged patina.

Briefly, the method works like this. First, the artist prepares a solution of turpentine mixed with a small amount of warm or cool oil color (depending on the desired tonal effect of the painting). Then, on a stretched sheet of watercolor paper, Bye takes a large brush and completely wets the paper so that the water tends to run off. He immediately dips an oil painting brush into the prepared oil-turpentine solution and spatters the color onto the wet paper. The color will want to run in all directions but, by tilting the board slightly up or down, the artist can direct and control the color to stay in certain desired areas. Before the paper begins to dry, this procedure can be repeated with a number of other oil and turpentine mixtures on the sky, ground, or tree areas of the painting.

After applying the underpainting, Bye lets the board dry overnight. In the following session, he removes any oil globules that might have remained on the paper; if the spattered color has produced too rich an effect, he washes out the area with soap and water to leave a remaining thin residue. This thinly tinted layer of paint forms the underpainting upon which the artist can proceed with his usual transparent watercolor technique. To what extent one wishes to wash out the oil-turps is a matter of personal preference.

No special technique is required to apply the wash over the oil underpainting, and sometimes Bye feels inclined to leave certain areas untouched altogether. He may use opaque watercolor or gouache to touch up highlights or to make corrections. Bye is careful to mask out beforehand the areas which he intends to treat in detail—in complex architectural compositions, for example—so that the oil and turpentine will not affect them. This kind of underpainting for a watercolor must be used with discretion.

Bye's watercolor palette consists of the following colors: Naples yellow, lemon yellow, cadmium yellow medium, yellow ochre or raw sienna, sepia (one of his favorites), sap green, oxide of chromium, viridian, cerulean blue, ultramarine, Prussian blue, Payne's gray, black, light red, cadmium red, alizarin crimson, mauve, and gouache white. This makes a rather large palette, but he seldom uses all of this list in every painting.

The artist paints with six assorted, fine quality sable brushes ranging from a no. 6 round to a 1½″ wide flat, which he likes for large washes. He carries all his materials in a metal fisherman's gear box. It contains a pen knife, razor blade, Kleenex, pencils, maskoid, and India ink. (He uses maskoid sparingly because he has found that it can cause the white area to yellow slightly within a year or two.) Bye prefers 300 lb rough paper for most subjects, but he also keeps on hand some cold pressed paper for special subjects. In the field, he uses a good watercolor easel.

W. R. Cameron

Rain Clouds
Watercolor 11¼″ x 15¼″

Wʜᴇɴ ᴡ. ʀ. ᴄᴀᴍᴇʀᴏɴ ᴡᴏʀᴋs on location—which he prefers, rather than working in his studio—he uses two paint boxes, the smaller containing paints, brushes, water bottle, rags, and watercolor pads; the larger box holding either stretched medium weight paper or very heavy rough stock. He places the large box on his knees, the top of which swings back to form an easel. A small folding stool completes the outfit. Sometimes he works in his car.

For materials, the artist prefers rough watercolor paper, although he finds charcoal paper quite suitable for small sketches (especially figure studies) and it combines well with brown ink drawings. He usually uses three sable brushes: no. 3 or 4, no. 8, and no. 12. Sometimes he substitutes a flat 1″ sable for the no. 12. The artist finds a ⅜″ to 1″ wide bristle brush useful for washing and lifting off unwanted color.

Cameron frequently uses the following colors on his palette: cadmium yellow light, yellow ochre, Indian or light red, English vermilion or cadmium red light, alizarin crimson, rose madder, ultramarine blue, cobalt blue, Prussian blue, viridian green, burnt umber, and ivory black.

First, the artist makes numerous thumbnail sketches for composition. Then he begins to paint, keeping the paper as wet as possible for more subjects. An atmospheric effect may be painted with totally wet paper. On the other hand, he uses a drier technique when he paints an architectural motif which requires detail, although he always strives for a liquid, spontaneous quality.

The artist feels that good drawing is essential to watercolor. Changes, he says, are practically impossible in this medium, since alterations kill the spontaneity of the work, especially in the use of pure transparent watercolor. If the drawing is good, it matters little whether the artist uses a pencil or charcoal, or begins to draw directly with the brush. (The last method is very valuable in capturing fleeting impressions, especially clouds and weather effects, but this technique requires real mastery of the medium.) When outdoor subjects are impractical, Cameron often does still life for practice in drawing, value study, and composition. The same principles apply to still life as to landscapes.

Because James Carlin travels a great deal, he is quite often compelled to adapt himself to conditions unfavorable to painting. Climate, terrain, and other factors frequently dictate his watercolor approach; consequently, his works are not always painted in the same manner. For instance, in Oaxaca, Mexico, he followed a child's funeral, painting as he walked. He tied a string around his neck and tacked it to both edges of the drawing in the manner of a sandwich board; in this way, he was able to walk and paint at the same time, using the dry brush method (carrying much water would have been too difficult). Another time, Carlin forgot his brushes and had to use his fingers as a substitute to apply the various patches of color.

When he travels, Carlin reduces his painting equipment to a minimum: a watercolor block, good quality, about 14" x 18" (blocks are efficient to transport and store); a folding aluminum stool; brushes (the best quality red sable) nos. 4, 6, 10, and a 12" flat; a small folding palette to which he attaches a tiny aluminum drinking cup for water; a water canteen; and sunglasses. He puts everything into a hiking pack and fastens it to his back, an arrangement that makes it easier for him to walk to his destination.

On location, Carlin paints directly with the brush, occasionally adding some Chinese white to make adjustments. Sometimes he makes several impressions of the same subject (using brush only). If details are necessary, he makes separate drawings in pencil on another piece of paper. With this material, he reconstructs and invents when he returns to his studio.

In his studio, Carlin uses 300 lb cold or hot pressed paper. After tacking the paper to a small drafting table, he wipes its surface with a sponge or damp rag. This procedure retains the texture, yet facilitates paint absorption. Next, using his travel impressions as a guide, he sketches the main masses in pencil. If figures are the prominent feature, he draws with more care, because it is an easy matter, when using watercolor, to ruin the work of hours in two minutes.

After blocking in the darks—never staying too long in the same area—he manipulates the masses until he arrives at a pleasing design. If he is satisfied, he allows it to dry, after which he proceeds to add color and strength where needed. Detail is left to last.

Carlin's watercolor palette consists of the following tube colors: cadmium yellow pale, yellow ochre, cadmium red light, alizarin crimson, burnt umber, burnt sienna, ultramarine blue, cerulean blue, viridian green, and phthalocyanine green. This rather limited palette provides a wide range of effects.

Tʜᴇ ᴀᴘᴘʀᴏᴀᴄʜ ᴄʟᴀʀᴇɴᴄᴇ ᴄᴀʀᴛᴇʀ ᴜꜱᴇꜱ for his painting varies with time, place, and other factors. For example, at one time, he wished to do night scenes of Pittsburgh subjects. To accomplish the desired effect, he worked with colored crayons and watercolor in a wax resist technique. He obtained a rich sparkle and quick interpretation of the night lights that one sees with such dramatic impact in Pittsburgh—the various lights that sparkle from the houses and streets clustering the hillsides, the bursts of fire from the Bessemer furnaces that flame into the night sky. The ribbons of red, yellow, green, and blue cutting across the rivers all lent themselves to the richness of colored crayons washed over with pure watercolor of deep, dark tones intensified with black. To get pure, clear light, he merely scraped here and there with a razor blade. This experiment was motivated by his desire to interpret what he saw and felt.

During the winter months on the Delaware River, the fresh sparkle of the snow in the fields around his studio challenged Carter to find a way to interpret its beauty. The glitter had eluded him previously. One evening he was talking with a friend about a new paper that was being developed. His friend brought him some samples of the paper which contained 75% glass fiber and were quite soft in texture. That paper was the answer to the problem.

Before painting *The Guardian Angel* (reproduced on the facing page), Carter found an old piece of warm-colored paper that he had stored away for a long time. It was so aged that he began to feel the antiquity of the subject as soon as he started to work. He took advantage of this mood and never lost it until he finished the painting. He used washes of gouache to build slowly toward the feeling that had been engendered by the old paper.

Francis Chapin

Elizabeth Hall No. 2
Watercolor 30" x 40"

W<small>HEN HE PAINTED OUTDOORS</small>, which he generally preferred, Francis Chapin (1899–1965) set up one easel in the shade and a second easel alongside it to hold his palette, water, and brushes. In *Elizabeth Hall No. 2* (reproduced on the facing page), he worked on a double-elephant all-rag paper which was trimmed down to fit a 30" x 40" frame. He always stretched his paper on a heavy corrugated board before working, an excellent stretching surface for large paper, available at most furniture stores. Chapin wet the paper on both sides with a sponge and then fastened it to the board, using strips of gummed paper.

Before he began to paint, Chapin always squared off the paper and divided the picture plane into geometric proportions, similar to the method of the *golden section* used by old masters. However, Chapin never made a preliminary drawing *of his subject* before he painted. A drawing would have lessened his spontaneity and discouraged any changes. However, he made countless drawings in a long series of sketchbooks.

Chapin used two metal compartmented trays for palettes, each about 8" x 14" with eleven divided sections on a side. He used one palette for the warm colors, the other for the cool. In the warm sections, he placed Hansa pale yellow, permanent yellow, cadmium yellow, yellow medium, cadmium yellow deep, cadmium orange, scarlet, permanent pink, cadmium red, alizarin crimson, Mars violet, light red, burnt sienna, raw sienna, yellow ochre, light green, citron. In the cool sections he put out manganese blue, cobalt blue, ultramarine blue, phthalocyanine blue, chrome oxide green, phthalocyanine green, Grignet's green, permanent violet, cobalt violet, Payne's gray, burnt umber, raw umber, and ivory black.

Before tackling the detail, Chapin laid in all-over washes in vibrant, sometimes complementary colors. He used many and varied tools. The brushes were all fitted in a 12" x 16" metal case and ran the gamut from sign writers' brushes of 1¼", a Japanese brush 3¼" wide for broad washes, to an assortment of red sables, sizes 10 to 16. Also used with interesting results were assorted bamboo sticks, and one large, hand-whittled pine stick that he manipulated skillfully to achieve a particular kind of calligraphy.

The painting of Elizabeth Hall took five "painting days" to complete. Chapin built slowly and carefully, maintaining a transparent freshness in spite of repeated over-all washes, scrapings, and jabs with bamboo sticks dipped in India ink for accented line. He painted instinctively, avoiding tricks and flashy effects. He often rescued a painting from the brink of disaster by using a brush handle or knife for scratching, or a dash of pastel to bring to life a deadened area.

54   Albert Christ-Janer

Sea Forms
Watercolor 19" x 23"

ALBERT CHRIST-JANER, in developing his distinctive watercolors, shuns a methodical technique; each painting evolves out of its own demands, is created in its own unique manner. He commands control by what he terms *trained instinct*—rather than by learned formulae—so that he is able to bring off any technical problem as it arises.

When he paints in watercolor, Christ-Janer makes constant use of polymer glue, an acrylic binding agent or medium. He uses the glue in all forms, thick and thin, to achieve various textural effects and to alter the consistency of his colors. After creating linear effects with Moore's white, an opaque paint, he mounts Japanese rice paper to a board—cardboard, gesso, or Masonite—using the polymer glue. He then textures the rice paper so that the surface is smooth in some areas, rough in others.

Placing the board on the floor, he constantly walks around his painting as he works. He applies the first layer of paint recklessly, using high intensity watercolors, and adding the thick polymer glue to his paints in various doses. Since he never uses the same technique twice, he may—at this time—add sand to his paints; or he may use powdered pigments (particularly in the earth colors) or high quality tube colors. He may apply paint with brushes (he favors large housepainters' brushes), or with a spatula, or using his hands or rags, or he may even let the paint spill over at random.

Christ-Janer also achieves interesting textural effects by soaking a second sheet of rice paper in paint and then pasting the wet paper to his painting surface with the polymer glue. Frequently he applies wax lines or repeats the opaque white lines which flow through masses of color, acting as a contrast to the other passages of the painting. Although his first application of paint is generally one of high intensity, the colors become gradually subdued by a succession of further layers —a kind of glazing technique.

Christ-Janer completes his paintings only after several sessions of work. One painting may take three months; another may not be completed for two years. He regards each painting as a growing process, involving various experimental and unplanned stages. He feels that any painting he has done which was pre-planned was a disaster. He stated, "The earth, the sky, and the sea are my sources of information; art is my inspiration. Combining the endless challenge of nature with the vast lessons of art, I try to make forms which will invite you to look, to contribute your vision to mine. If you become involved with what this vision turns out to be, you will be absorbed in my work. My best expectation is that you will enjoy making this work your own discovery."

56   Ruth Cobb

Ruth Cobb

Autumn Gold
Watercolor 20¾″ x 29½″
Collection, Shore Gallery

Rᴜᴛʜ ᴄᴏʙʙ ɪs ɪɴsᴘɪʀᴇᴅ by the textures and patterns of nature, the endless variations of growing things, and ordinary, familiar objects in sunlight and in shade. In warm weather, she sketches outdoors—but never does a *finished* painting in the field. She collects items of all kinds which she uses for subject matter when painting in her studio: stones and shells, feathers, birds' nests, branches, objects of colored glass (bottles, goblets, and fragments of fine stained glass). In the fall, she gathers dried weeds and grasses from weed patches and river banks: milkweed down, seed pods, and Queen Anne's lace.

Before painting, Ruth Cobb thinks a great deal about the subject, composition, and color. There is usually some special feature or quality that she tries to emphasize: sometimes it is pattern, sometimes a color scheme, sometimes a luminescence. Generally, she makes a small, rough sketch in pastel or Conté crayon to quickly set down a particular idea for emphasis, and to make the proportions of the composition final. The best study for her purpose is deliberately rough and unfinished, because she finds too complete a sketch inhibiting.

At the outset, the artist determines the color scheme. Although she does not follow any scientific formula, she does decide whether the color will be warm or cool, delicate or bold. Some of her best paintings have been simply variations of browns and grays. Sometimes a whole painting idea will emerge as she decides to use only a gamut of reds.

The artist starts by stretching the paper on a plywood board and securing it on all sides with paper tape. While the paper is still wet, she freely brushes in the complete subject, allowing the colors to run together at random. The painting is then put away until the next day. With the paper tight as a drum and thoroughly dry, she continues with flat, clear washes which usually do not completely hide the softly blurred color beneath. At this time, the tonalities can be adjusted, contrasts heightened, and shapes made clearer. Sometimes she draws on this color base with a pen, brush, or stub. Occasionally, she scrapes away white lines with a razor blade, since the fine grade of paper she uses will take limited corrections without harm.

Her favorite paper is a heavy, smooth-surfaced English brand. (She does not care for the mechanical effects of rough papers.) She has also used French colored papers that may initiate many unexpected color schemes—though this paper is fragile and requires special care in handling. She also has done some watercolors on stretched canvas covered with a gesso ground. This method interests her because the gesso is less absorbent than paper and makes the color seem more brilliant. From time to time, she uses a combination of opaque casein and transparent watercolor to produce a feeling of depth.

WHEN KENT DAY COES WORKS OUTDOORS in the winter, he uses a 10″ x 14″ block of 140 lb cold pressed paper which he holds in his lap, in his car. In more clement weather, he stands at a watercolor easel, the board level or almost so, his water jar on a stool beside him. Then he works on single sheets previously stretched, in sizes up to 18″ x 25″, on either rough or cold pressed paper. Coes firmly believes that the watercolorist should be able to adapt his technique to the different weights and surfaces of paper, exploiting the advantages of each.

Frequently, these smaller sketches, though treated on the spot as complete small paintings, are the basis of larger works made in the studio. He may enlarge a single sketch, or—as happens more often—he may combine several into a single composition.

When Coes paints a railroad subject—such as the one illustrated here—he starts with an idea, perhaps a memory of something barely glimpsed in passing. He finally translates these mental images into a final painting, by the following method: first, he develops his composition by sketching out the subject on a 6″ x 9″ sheet of layout tracing paper, using a 6B carpenter's pencil. These sketches contain only flat tones and atmosphere, with very little detail. By doing many of these quick sketches—often referring to photographs of trains in action—the artist is able to establish the design, which is the basis of a successful painting.

Coes then selects a final pencil composition and enlarges it by redrawing on a sheet of tracing paper to the size desired for the watercolor, drawing in only the outlines with an HB pencil. Adjustments in design are made at this stage. Once the drawing is transferred to the watercolor paper, the design is secure.

Up to this point, no color has been involved. Although he squeezes out twenty-four colors, Coes uses only a few in any one painting. In beginning to paint from his black-and-white sketch, he allows his imagination to suggest the colors. The mixing area of his standard watercolor box is augmented by a plain white oval platter, about 12″ long.

Coes does most of his painting with four brushes of the very best quality: no. 7 and no. 12 round, and a ½″ and a ¼″ flat. For softening edges, when necessary, he uses a ¼″ flat bristle oil painter's brush. In addition to these brushes, the artist always keeps a few others in case of unusual circumstances.

Robert E. Conlan

Hudson River Gothic
Watercolor   19" x 26½"

Whenever possible, robert conlan prefers to paint on location, because he feels that the mood of the motif and his reaction to the surrounding area are of vital importance to the production of a good painting. His actual painting procedure is a combination of the wet and dry techniques, the proportion of wet to dry depending on the effect he wishes to create.

For ease of handling, Conlan often stretches his paper. Although he varies weights and textures, he usually prefers the 140 lb, hot pressed finish—an unusual choice for watercolor, but permitting good control. His palette is a butcher's tray that has Lucite divisions with spaces for twenty colors. It cleans easily and provides ample space for mixing. The cover of the palette is black plastic, hinged onto the tray. Conlan's brushes are mainly red sables of different sizes and shapes, ranging from a no. 2 to no. 6. Since he enjoys varying his technique, he often alternates his tools.

A case in point is the painting, *Hudson River Gothic*, reproduced on the facing page. It was painted in a sunlit area providing little or no shade, which necessitated a hurried procedure, for paint has a tendency to harden and dry quickly under such conditions. First, he developed the basic composition in a series of small sketches which disregarded detail, emphasizing value patterns only. Then he made a large linear drawing on watercolor paper and shifted, added, or eliminated various elements in order to create a cohesive composition.

To achieve unity of color, the artist decided that the over-all feeling dictated a cool dominance. Conlan applied the basic washes of sky and background first, leaving the center of interest to the last. The entire painting took approximately three hours. His interpretation here is primarily realistic. He wanted to capture the dilapidated charm of the station itself, and this called for a traditional approach. However, if he were to undertake the same subject again, he stated that it might well be painted in a different manner.

Fire Tug
Watercolor 5¾" x 16"
Collection, Mrs. Crosby Glendening

Hereward lester cooke's technique is a surprising combination of two forces: the controlled accident and exceptional attention to detail.

Cutting a long, thin rectangle from a 22" x 30" sheet of good rag paper (his paintings are rarely more than 22" wide), Cooke drops the sheet into the bathtub and soaks it for ten minutes. He then places the sheet carefully in the center of a large blotter, leaving wide margins of blotter on all sides. Next he places the blotter on a large sheet of flexible cardboard. This is Cooke's drawing board.

Onto the wet sheet of watercolor paper, Cooke squeezes pure color directly from the tube to develop a satisfying abstract design. With a big no. 12 round red sable, he begins to manipulate the blobs and blurs, moving them in one direction or another, thinning them into washes, picking out light passages with a clean brush that lifts wet color. He picks up the flexible cardboard and curves it and tilts it to control the flow of color. At this stage, the watercolor looks like a small abstract painting: no subject, just blobs and blurs of strong color moving on the glistening, wet surface. (Cooke uses 140 lb paper, inclined to curl as it dries, but he refuses to stretch the paper, tape its edges, or even tack it down; the curling plays its own part in the accidental flow of color.)

To speed drying of a passage he likes and wants to preserve, Cooke fires a blast of hot air from a gun-shaped hair dryer. To slow the drying of a passage that needs more work and threatens to solidify too soon, he turns to a bubbling tea kettle which sends forth a jet of steam to moisten the paper.

The dried abstraction now goes into a drawer or a closet, where it joins scores of similar blurry action paintings. Looking at the interplay of abstract forms and colors six months later, Cooke begins to "discover" his subject as it begins to congeal into shapes of a landscape, an architectural view, a coastal scene. Now the artist begins to thumb through his thousands of sketches of landscape motifs —buildings, trees, rock formations, boats, bridges, lighthouses, clouds.

Working with small, round sable brushes, as small as no. oo, Cooke subtly molds the abstract forms into recognizable subject matter. He works for progressively greater detail as the painting nears completion. The brushes get smaller and smaller. He may even reach for a pen and black or colored inks. A cut-down bristle brush may be used to roughen and darken a passage. In its final stages, the watercolor may become a mixed media painting.

Cooke's palette is divided into two groups of colors, reflecting the two phases of the painting procedure. The early abstract phase is done entirely in the most transparent hues: ultramarine blue, burnt sienna, ivory black, viridian, yellow ochre, alizarin crimson, and Payne's gray. For the second phase—the naturalistic details superimposed on the abstraction—Cooke turns to the stronger, more opaque hues: cadmium yellow, Naples yellow, cerulean blue, Prussian blue, cadmium red, and sometimes Chinese white.

Houseboat, Tokyo Canal
Watercolor 19½" x 37"
Collection, The Metropolitan Museum of Art

WHEN MARIO COOPER sees a subject which suggests a possible motif, he quickly makes a pen sketch. Then he may make a color sketch and, if possible, further studies. He also takes photos with his two Leicas, one for color and the other in black and white. His color sketches are little abstractions which, for him, are like houses without people: a good place for a picture to happen. All the sketches are edited in his studio, and those that show promise are put in a priority folder.

For *Houseboat, Tokyo Canal*, reproduced here, he made dozens of preliminary sketches over a period of two years, some in pen and ink, to organize the linear rhythm, and some in color. The final sketch is about 6" wide, the size of the projector that he used to blow up the sketch to the size of a 22" x 30" sheet of paper. Not all his paintings take as long to produce; some are complete after one session, others may take years.

Most of Cooper's on-the-spot sketches are painted wet-in-wet. He soaks only one side of the sheet, using a 1" bristle and ox hair houspainter's brush rather than a sponge, since the brush lays a more even film. A sketch on a block of 140 lb paper may be finished without rewetting, adding some accents on the dry paper.

When painting a large picture, Cooper wets the paper in sections, like a fresco. The sky is saturated, leaving the other areas dry, and then painted while still wet; the same process is repeated for the other areas. After the paper is dry, some sections can be dampened again and repainted without destroying the freshness of the painting. Once the picture is virtually finished, he places it in a mat on an easel for several days of observation before he makes any changes. If they are not too extensive, adjustments can be made without losing the freshness. Quite often, he will paint the proposed change on a separate piece of paper and tip it on lightly with Scotch tape. Then, if it is suitable, but the area is already saturated with paint, he scrubs out the original color—an operation calling for patience and care—and repaints it.

For major paintings, Cooper usually uses a 300 lb paper stretched on a piece of three-ply board and stapled along the edge at two-inch intervals. His paints are tube colors: lemon yellow, cadmium yellow pale, cadmium yellow deep, Indian yellow, cadmium orange, cadmium scarlet, cadmium red deep, scarlet, alizarin crimson, rose madder genuine, burnt sienna, burnt umber, raw sienna, raw umber, phthalocyanine green, violet, ultramarine blue, and Payne's gray, arranged on his palette in the order listed. He does not use black because, when mixed, he feels that it has a tendency to muddy other colors.

For brushes, Cooper uses the flat sable brights, nos. 20, 18, and 16, seldom requiring smaller sizes than these three. Occasionally, a 1½", 1", or ½" bristle or ox hair brush is useful for covering larger areas. He believes that a round sable holds too much water for his needs and that the square brush is easier to clean.

66   John E. Costigan

Group of Bathers
Watercolor and gouache   20" x 27½"

JOHN COSTIGAN PAINTS THE MAJORITY of his watercolors from drawings. In his bathing group subjects—such as the one reproduced here—he first makes a number of large drawings in the same size as the final watercolor. In all this figure work, he draws from memory. After he has visualized the pose and action on his drawing, he checks the proportions and details with a model. (His wife and children have been constant models.) In these drawings—made with a Conté crayon or brush and ink—Costigan keeps changing the grouping until he is satisfied that he has achieved a good composition. With this in hand, he then makes several careful drawings of each of the main figures, and from all these sketches he paints his watercolor. Sometimes he works on several sheets until he gets one that has good, clear color. He uses the transparent pigments mixed with white whenever he thinks he can get better color quality by its addition.

In landscape pictures, he usually features one interesting tree or group of trees and builds his picture around it. Figures are added in the picture whenever he feels they will add interest to the subject. A small figure well placed gives a feeling of scale to the trees.

For most of his watercolors, Costigan prefers to work on a 300 lb rough-surfaced paper, especially for figure groups and landscapes. In painting directly from the model—often portrait studies of his children—he finds a hot pressed sheet works best for him. His palette and choice of brushes are the usual ones but, like most artists, he varies them according to his needs.

Staats Cotsworth

Freight Trains
Casein 30" x 24"
Collection, Muriel Kirkland

Staats cotsworth uses regular tube casein paints on either Masonite or heavy illustration board which has been prepared with a gesso ground. His formula for this ground is as follows: To a half pint of warm liquid gesso, he adds raw sienna (casein) and a two-ounce jigger of casein varnish (obtainable at any art shop). He applies three coats with a soft camel's hair brush, allowing them to dry thoroughly, sanding these with fine sandpaper between coats. The surface of most ready-made gesso panels is too absorbent for him, and although some have an interesting "tooth," Cotsworth resurfaces them anyway to vary the rough and smooth areas to suit his subject. The raw sienna gives him a golden warmth on which to build a chiaroscuro with raw umber in the early stages of painting.

Cotsworth's palette consists of the siennas, umbers, and alizarin crimson with occasional use of phthalocyanine blue and green. He finds it necessary to spray varnish on each glaze in order to see what he has painted. For this he uses ethereal or casein varnish cut in half with alcohol, which brings out the natural color without becoming too glossy.

Cotsworth manipulates his paints in semi-transparent washes—like watercolor—or in built-up layers of opaque pigment, much like oil paint. This is a particularly rewarding method, because the vibrant textures of aging wood and crumbling stone are best suggested with the sort of luminosity that only the transparent techniques can achieve. Like all such media, casein calls for planning and patience. To know where to use the paint as a thin wash or juicy impasto requires thorough familiarity with the distinctive properties of casein as well as a carefully conceived attack. So adept is this artist that he can stop in the middle of a picture and put aside his painting for months or even years—numerous projects are usually humming at one time—and return to his half-completed picture knowing exactly what comes next. The casein painter must always be sure of his direction: there can be no trusting to luck. Otherwise, he ends up with a heavily painted picture that will crack and chip or will be murky and dull.

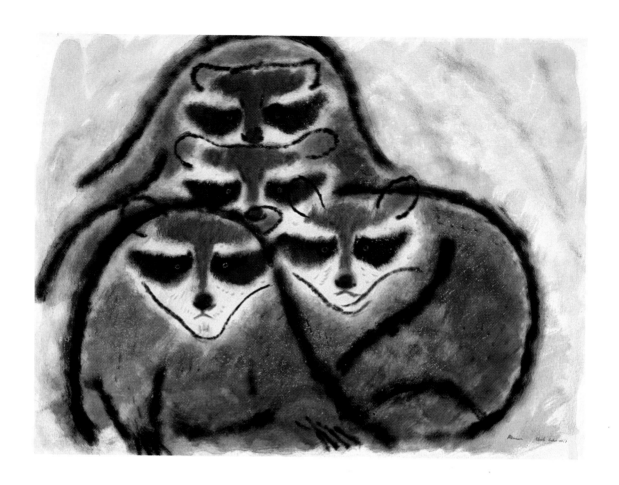

70 Charles Culver

CHARLES CULVER (1908–1967) SKETCHED HIS SUBJECT—usually animals, birds, insects, or flowers—from life, adding written notations of color and value. Later he *painted* in the studio. Sometimes the idea was clear at the outset, and the painting developed quickly and easily. At other times, there may have been a succession of additional drawings, color studies, or studies for arrangement before the idea clarified itself. In painting moths and butterflies, he often found it helpful to make careful, factual, preliminary studies of wing and body structures; and of designs and markings on both body and wings. Then, finally, the idea may have become clear—a distillation of facts, ideas, and feelings. If the process was complete, the pictures came off quickly. If not, then he found further experimentation necessary. If, after several days of struggling, no clear idea presented itself, he lay the problem aside to take up something else. Often weeks or months passed —occasionally a year or more—before he took it up again. Sooner or later, however, the idea appeared and then he painted, rather deliberately, but at the same time quite rapidly.

Culver painted only in transparent watercolors. He seldom used opaques, although occasionally he added a bit of white to a color to achieve a desired effect. Sometimes he plastered on transparent color very thickly to reach a correct value, to find a proper level of intensity, or to achieve a satisfactory substance. His brushes were bristle—such as oil painters use. With these brushes, he applied the color to the paper as though rubbing it into the surface. His palette was an old porcelain-topped kitchen table with legs sawed off to a comfortable height. Culver stood or sat before an easel, with watercolor paper held upright on a board by tape at the corners. He used a full range of colors on the palette, including the extremities of black and white. (As a rule, the white of the paper was the only white employed.) All weights and surfaces of fine watercolor paper were used, including the thinner papers.

Raccoons, reproduced here, was one of the paintings that went swiftly through its necessary stages from sketch to final execution. (It was completed in slightly more than two hours.) It is most economical in color, employing only raw sienna, burnt umber, ivory black, and a small amount of neutralized ultramarine blue.

Although he approached each painting in a slightly different way, Culver used fairly common methods with this one. First, a full-sized graphite study was sketched on a large sheet of watercolor paper. Then, an all-over tone of a rather cool gray was scumbled over the sketch. While this was still damp, he blotted the areas of the animals' faces to lighten them, and rubbed in a very light tint of raw sienna. All of the lighter tones were put in first and the heavy black notes, suggesting the outlines of the animals' bodies, last. The little wavy lines were scratched out with a palette knife.

72   Edwin L. Dahlberg

End of the Cape
Watercolor 21" x 29"

ALL OF EDWIN DAHLBERG'S WATERCOLORS are actual scenes painted from nature. He may move a tree or avoid a tangent, but he does not invent a picture, and if he makes too many changes he feels that the genuineness and honesty are lost. He works directly, striving to put the color down in its correct value the first time with a loaded brush, because he feels that every additional flick destroys its freshness to some degree.

Dahlberg likes to work simply, and uses only three brushes, getting most use from a no. 12 of the finest red sable—one that points well and holds a good quantity of color. According to the artist, quality brushes are an absolute must, and the moment they lose their point he discards them. The other two brushes he employs are a no. 6 and a no. 2 for more detailed work, as the sketch is brought to a finish. Sometimes he uses a razor blade, but he tries to execute a job without it, and he seldom uses any opaque color.

The artist's standard palette consists of Naples yellow, lemon yellow, cadmium yellow pale, vermilion, alizarin crimson, cobalt blue, ultramarine, Prussian blue, and Hooker's green 1 and 2, which he places in a series of wells on one side of a white butcher's tray. On the other side of the tray, he places the "earth" series: yellow ochre, light red, burnt sienna, burnt umber, sepia, Payne's gray, and black. He prefers a restricted palette.

Dahlberg never makes preliminary sketches for composition and arrangement, because he is emotionally keyed up while he paints and prefers to express his feeling directly on paper, rather than dissipate his energy in preliminary work. He would rather take a chance on the painting turning out a failure—in which case he discards it and starts it all over again. He feels that he learns so much from the first attempt that most problems are solved by the second time around, leaving him free to splash into it uninhibitedly.

The artist generally prefers cold pressed or rough paper—either 140 lb, soaked and mounted, or 300 lb unmounted. If the projected picture is small, he uses a slightly smoother surface. After the paper is mounted, he roughs in the various units of his composition in pencil outline. In most cases, he works on dry paper, although if he wants a soft effect in doing the sky he wets that part of the paper and works into it before it dries. (*End of the Cape* is an exception to his usual procedure: here he worked on a completely wet paper in order to capture the mood of the late afternoon on a damp, foggy day.)

Dahlberg paints the sky first (he has even painted the sky with a sponge), and then he works all over the paper, often putting in the darkest dark next so that he can judge the range of values. He tries to bring the entire picture to completion simultaneously. Parts that may not look finished while he is painting often surprise him by taking their place without further work, thus helping to preserve the fresh, free look he tries to attain.

74   John DeTore

Structures

Watercolor 17½″ x 23½″

W HEN JOHN DETORE PAINTS in a *traditional* technique, he uses three or four high quality round sables, a ¾″ bristle, and a sky mop. His palette contains alizarin crimson, cadmium yellow light, Indian yellow, barium yellow, cadmium red, Hooker's green dark, phthalocyanine green and blue, cobalt blue, new blue, mauve, Payne's gray, yellow ochre, and burnt umber. He paints on 140 lb rough paper stretched on ½″ plywood; he blots the paper with a turkish towel and staples it with an office stapler, one staple per inch. Before painting, DeTore always makes several miniature preliminary sketches. He enlarges one of the designs onto a sheet of watercolor paper by using the squared system, employing pencil for guidelines only.

The technique used in painting *Structures* is an example of an unusual departure from the traditional manner of working, which constitutes a good auxiliary to the familiar method. The technique requires a 3″ wide painter's roller made of mohair, and rectangular fiber sponges, 4″ x 6″, which may be purchased for a few cents apiece. For paper, he uses a heavy ply, fine grain stock, though he also gets interesting results from the texture of good quality mat board.

First, the artist soaks the sponges with several predominant colors, one color per sponge, and then places them on an impervious surface (he uses light gauge tin). He runs the roller over the sponges to pick up color, the amount of which can be controlled by varying the pressure of the roller. He then applies the color to any finely grained paper which has been taped to a piece of Masonite. To avoid rubbing into the previous layer, he allows the paint to dry after the first application before applying a second color film. With this precaution, the color does not become muddy, and as many as four or five separate layers may be added. To make linear strokes, DeTore impresses the edge of the roller onto the paper. After the first or second application has dried, by rewetting the surface with clean water, the artist can push the paint around or scrape it with a 1″ pliable putty knife, the corners of which have been rounded and highly polished. For example, one small stroke will scrape out the window of a building and the paint thus gathered may be used to draw the window bars or to produce some other detail.

DeTore has found that squeezing a tube of watercolor into a four-ounce plastic bottle, adding a ball bearing and shaking hastens its solution. Then he can quickly squirt the pigment, diluted with water, onto the sponge. (He keeps several bottles of color on hand.) The bottles are also invaluable for painting with a brush. When he does use a brush in conjunction with the roller, he runs a clean roller over the brushwork to retain the rolled effect.

On *Structures*, he also used "printings" (engraved art gum) to add to the detail around the signs over the old store fronts. As a last addition to this technique, he generally sprays the painting with a dull acrylic lacquer to improve the surface structure and intensify the pigments applied.

Edwin Fulwider

Clearwater River, Idaho
Watercolor 20" x 28"
Collection, Dr. and Mrs. John D. Millett

Edwin fulwider paints exclusively on the spot, regardless of the weather. Once he has selected a subject (perhaps making one or two thumbnail sketches), he blocks in the composition roughly with a 2B pencil to locate the large forms and main lines. Details are drawn directly with the brush, not with the pencil. Next, he sponges the sheet thoroughly to remove most of the graphite, leaving only a faint trace of the drawing and at the same time providing a wet surface to drop in the first big masses of color—bright, clear, and intense. He uses lots of paint in the brush and does all the mixing on the wet paper. As these colors dry, he hardens edges where necessary. The painting is well along by the first drying, though some areas may be left blank at this stage to receive more careful drawing later with the brush.

With the first wet stage complete, he next lays in the flat areas of color that may require a hard edge. He then adds details and lines, either on dry paper, or by rewetting the area with clear water and dropping additional color in the right place. The artist often uses a straightedge with the brush to keep the architectural quality of the building crisp in contrast to the soft quality of the landscape. At the detail stage, he sometimes uses a little opaque tempera white to bring out highlights and to sharpen buildings and linear elements. This whole painting procedure requires an hour to an hour and a half of intense work. Returning to his studio, Fulwider adds some further finish and perhaps makes a minor change or two.

The artist uses only the best quality tube watercolors, putting them on the palette fresh each time he paints. His palette consists of ivory black, phthalocyanine blue, phthalocyanine green, cobalt blue, cadmium red light, cadmium yellow light, yellow ochre, alizarin crimson, burnt umber, Payne's gray, and a tempera white. Sometimes he also adds burnt sienna, raw sienna, manganese blue, cerulean blue, cadmium yellow medium, and cadmium red medium. For a palette, he uses a small, partitioned, enameled white tin tray. He buys the cheapest kind in quantity and discards them after a few sessions.

Most of his brushwork is done with a 1" flat red sable of the best quality. For detail work, he uses round ferrule lettering brushes, nos. 3, 7, and 8, and several small round watercolor brushes, nos. 1, 2, 4, and 7.

A small, homemade box holds all of his painting equipment. For a painting stand, he uses a homemade folding, tripod-supported table that can be adjusted to any terrain. His watercolor paper is held with four paper clips to a piece of corrugated cardboard cut to 23" x 31", one inch larger all around than his full sheet of 100% rag watercolor paper. In case of high winds at the site, the cardboard holding the paper is clamped to the table top with two C clamps.

78   Hertha Furth

Soukh of the Coppersmiths, Fez
Watercolor 13" x 16"
Collection, Mrs. Martin M. Philipsborn, Jr.

Hertha furth always carries at least a few materials in her pocket or hand-bag in order to jot down fleeting impressions. At times, she has even used pencil stubs, fountain pens, burnt matches, lipstick, face powder, and coffee grounds on such surfaces as shopping bags, newspapers, and paper napkins. Normally, however, she chooses the best available sable brushes in various widths according to what she plans to paint. She prefers wide, wedge-shaped brushes, and she always employs a plump, round no. 2 with a fine point for linear accents. The artist also uses a small sponge to soften hard edges or to transfer the color on the palette directly to the paper.

At times the artist uses a "resist" in her painting, either wax crayon or beeswax, to give interesting textural effects. She does not advocate their use to accomplish haphazard or clever areas, but she does find them desirable in carefully planned passages. She recommends experimenting first on scraps of various textured papers in order to decide which paper and resist will best suit one's purpose. Using heavy paper—which can withstand punishment—she floods ink over the whole sheet with the finished resist and watercolor painting, then immediately giving it a bath of cold water and working over it with rags, razor, and sponge, putting in accents of chalk or ink.

When working in her studio, she uses two white enamel palettes: one for warm, the other for cool colors. Her palette contains cadmium yellow, cadmium orange, vermilion, cerulean blue, cobalt blue, French ultramarine, yellow ochre, burnt sienna, raw umber, Payne's gray, alizarin crimson, viridian, and Winsor green and blue. Occasionally, she adds manganese blue and Winsor red. Both in the studio and when traveling, she keeps a choice of several papers on hand so that she can select one to suit the character of the subject. Generally, she paints on a 140 lb English or French paper in a smooth finish. She also uses various tinted papers which lend themselves to gouache and mixed techniques.

This inventive artist has developed a convenient method of carrying her supplies with her when traveling. Because of the difficulties in finding suitable paper when traveling abroad, the artist now takes along a lightweight plywood board cut to fit the bottom of her suitcase. She selects enough paper to last the duration of her trip, cut to the same size as the board, and packs the sheets flat on top of the plywood, along with one 12" x 18" spiral pad and two or three smaller sizes. She finds transparent zippered cosmetic bags very practical for transporting her supply of watercolors. She also carries a lightweight rectangular white enamel palette and a roll of heavy aluminum foil to cover the remaining colors left over in the wells after the day's work. (A drop of water the next day, out of an eyedropper, renders them workable again.) Another plastic bag contains one or two bottles of ink, pens, bamboo quills, Japanese swizzle sticks, and felt pens for a variety of thin or wide graphic accents; also a pen knife.

Henry Gasser

Old Granville Farm
Watercolor 19" x 25"

IN HIS WORK, HENRY GASSER ISOLATES various painting problems, concentrating for a time, let us say, on winter landscape. Then he works out the problems inherent to the particular subject. At the time he painted *Old Granville Farm*, reproduced here, he was experimenting with a low-keyed palette, letting the unpainted patches of white paper become intrinsic parts of the major design.

Although many of his exhibition watercolors have been painted in the studio, he always refers to notes made on the spot. The notes may consist of anything from just a fragmentary pencil sketch to several detailed drawings noting design, the balance of light and dark, and so forth. A small watercolor painted "color for color" on-the-spot may supplement these drawings. *Old Granville Farm* was produced in the studio. He had made about a dozen sketches of the farm from various angles, and from these he made three finished studio paintings.

Gasser has, in the past, employed a method of using his sketches which he has found successful. He works from a small drawing made in outline with penciled notations of color. He places a sheet of tracing paper over the outline drawing and indicates the values with the broadside of the pencil. Combining the two, he will be able to make a finished watercolor in the quiet of his studio. He developed this method through necessity while he was in the army, carrying a small 5" x 8" pad of semi-transparent paper with him at all times.

Generally, Henry Gasser uses a 140 lb rough or cold pressed 22" x 30" paper for finished work. He works dry, occasionally wetting a section of the paper where blending is desired. He applies the paint directly, washing or sponging out a part if it helps to produce an interesting texture.

In doing a winter landscape, Gasser often uses a grayed greenish-blue wash and paints the entire picture with this mixture. He leaves the white paper for the light area, the wash representing the middle and dark masses. At this stage, the watercolor resembles a monochrome. Gasser then paints in the dark masses, using as much color as possible. Local color is added in the light where needed, but he depends upon the darks to carry the design. As much detail as he finds necessary can then be suggested to finish the painting.

Gasser's palette varies according to the subject, but he generally uses from eight to twelve colors. They are cadmium yellow, light and deep; cadmium red light; yellow ochre; burnt sienna; alizarin crimson; Indian red; French ultramarine; viridian; Payne's gray; and ivory black. Colors such as cerulean blue, vermilion, Davy's gray, and ochre are very helpful in controlling a wash when he works on a wet surface. These pigments are not too finely ground and will hold to the area to which they are applied, not running all over the paper.

Gasser uses tube colors with enough squeezed into the pans of his paint box at all times. He finds that moist colors are much easier to handle. Sable brushes, nos. 17, 6, and 3, plus a ½" flat, complete his equipment.

82   John Gould

W

HAT KIND OF SUBJECT MATTER is most suitable for watercolor? For John Gould, the subject must present good contrasts of light and dark and strong patterns usually found in late afternoon or early evening. Dramatic night lighting also fascinates him, and his studio paintings are often done from sketches made under street lights. Stormy day scenes—which he sketches in the comfort of his car—are ideal for his studio work.

Outdoor painting requires efficient equipment and Gould has given considerable attention to this area of organization. To keep color fresh and clean, he carries at least *three* lightweight plastic palettes, designed with many paint wells. Into these, he squeezes liberal amounts of the finest quality tube paint. Nor is he sparing in the number of sable brushes he carries, preferring to use fresh ones instead of taking time out to rinse and clean paint-laden brushes. A strong outdoor sketching easel (on which he places a large portfolio) holds his full sheet of rough, 300 lb paper. On windy days, he uses heavy clips to secure this support. He takes two folding stools—one to sit on and the other to hold extra palettes, brushes, and other materials.

After he has selected a subject, Gould blocks in the basic linear design with pencil, avoiding details, except for complicated structural areas which require carefully plotted perspective. The sky usually receives his first attention. First, he wets the paper in this area, using a large squirrel hair mop to create soft, loose, drippy effects.

When he needs a color, he mixes an ample amount of paint in the central spaces of the palette, to cover the entire area. But before applying any color mixture, Gould tests it on trial strips of the same paper stock he is using for his watercolor.

For most painting, Gould prefers the no. 10 or 12 pointed sable brush, but he also uses broad, flat sables for certain solid effects. To produce various surfaces, he employs passages of dry-brush and line, working with these on dry areas without resorting to opaque color.

Although he enjoys painting on location, there are certain subjects that seem to require more deliberation to develop, and these he paints in the studio, working from on-the-spot studies made in both monochrome and color. Here he plots the entire design more carefully than in his outdoor method, by making a linear cartoon in pencil on tracing paper and then transferring its image onto the watercolor support. With this solid foundation, he is free to carry out the painting as slowly or as rapidly as both time and situation dictate.

84   Frank Guttridge

ALTHOUGH HE HAS PAINTED on half sheets, working directly before his subject, Frank Guttridge now depends on small sketches rendered in pencil and ink. Using a bottle of black ink, a bottle of watered-down ink to make a gray, and a small brush, the artist makes his sketches on heavy typewriter paper clipped to a Masonite board. All around the edges of his drawing, he makes notations about the color, time of day, and atmosphere of his subject.

From these sketches, Guttridge plans and designs his watercolors. He makes a new composition in pencil, pulling everything together into four simple values, carefully placing the lights and darks. Material from several sketches may go into the final design—a house or barn from one, a tree or hill from another. When several of these compositions are finished, Guttridge studies the notations on the edge of the sketches and tries out the colors. He puts aside the color notations and the final pencil sketches until he feels able to paint a fresh watercolor. This may be the following morning or afternoon or next week; but when it happens, he paints and keeps on painting until he is satisfied.

Guttridge keeps several stretched sheets of paper on hand. He usually cuts a sheet of 140 lb cold pressed watercolor paper—not quite in half—to provide a piece 18″ x 22″. This is soaked in a tub for ten to fifteen minutes, then pressed out on a plywood board with a dry towel. He fastens down the edges on the plywood with a 2″ heavy gummed paper, the kind used for parcel post packages. This is stapled every 3″ for extra strength, in order to assure a positive stretch.

On this stretched and dried-out sheet, Guttridge draws his design with a 1B pencil. Then he sponges the whole sheet, with the board tilted a bit, from the top. He begins the painting with a wash of the color most suitable to the scheme of his whole subject, but in which he takes care not to cover the whites in his composition. The basic tone may be a gray or yellow ochre, or both, one washed over the other while very wet. He then works all of the soft underlying tones into the damp sheet, using a flat 2″ varnish brush, beginning with the large simple shapes, then working all over the entire picture to keep it moving. In this fashion, the artist is able to stay ahead of the drying, since each brushful of color adds new moisture to the paper. As the sheet dries, Guttridge develops the central part of the picture, using his largest round brush fully charged with color. He mixes his color on the paper, rather than on the palette, rolling the board to achieve a pleasing texture and to run the warm and cool colors together. His favorite color scheme is yellow ochre, burnt sienna, and black. His palette is French ultramarine blue, Winsor blue, aureolin yellow, yellow ochre, vermilion, burnt sienna, alizarin crimson, and ivory black.

When the whole sheet is about dry, little touches of dark are put in for accents, some dry-brush for texture, and a line here and there for definition. With the sheet still attached to the board, he puts on a trial mat to evaluate his efforts.

86   Richard Haines

Winter Rain
Watercolor 18" x 25"
Collection, California National Water Color Society

Richard Haines seldom does on-the-spot watercolors. When out sketching, he has more fun doing little thumbnail impressions—sometimes with a fountain pen, or pen and color—or just small watercolors ranging from 2" x 3" up to 5" x 7". He often makes ten or a dozen sketches around one subject. He tacks these onto his studio wall. If, after a period of reflection and reviewing, the sketches fit into a plan that intrigues him, he proceeds with the larger painting. He finds this procedure allows him to give more consideration to the arrangement of colored lines and planes he wishes to put down on paper. The final painting is usually made from a number of these small sketches which had only a casual relationship to each other at the time they were painted.

Because he believes the result justifies the means, Haines uses ink and watercolor together—color over wax crayons, and some opaques—scratching or scrubbing the paper, or trying any other method used by watercolorists. All he asks is that the result have unity.

Haines prefers using long-handled brushes, sable and bristle, and usually works standing, with the paper stretched on the top of the drawing table. His palette consists of black, two blues, two reds, three greens, and four earth colors. He uses various papers, including bond and smooth inking paper, and he has painted a number of watercolors on rice paper.

The painting reproduced here, *Winter Rain*, emerged from many preliminary sketches—horizontal, vertical, light, dark, with color variations. Haines painted it on a rough 200 lb paper. He used charcoal lines to indicate the large color planes. Next he made a few sweeps of wax across the paper at the angle of falling rain. Then he dampened the paper and applied the color in large washes, darkening it here, intensifying an area there, using line to suggest form and motion. As the paper became less moist, the darker, sharper lines were added. When the idea was realized to his satisfaction, he stopped working and signed it. The time involved in the actual painting was comparatively short—perhaps 45 minutes!

Vincent A. Hartgen

Snow Cascade
Watercolor 21½" x 29½"

Vincent hartgen uses only professional tube paints which he squeezes into jar lids fastened to a metal tray. He arranges his colors in a palette with earths, yellows, and reds at one end, blending toward blues and greens at the other. His palette is large—containing some forty different colors. He paints on a high grade paper, preferably handmade rag, rough or smooth, 72 to 140 lb in weight.

Hartgen never works on his final paintings in the field. Rather, he makes extensive impression-like sketches on the site, using pastel, crayon, or chalk. He often makes dozens of sketches of the same scene to capture the essence of the details. Later, in the studio, he studies these sketches while he is still able to recreate the sum total of his *impression*—not the scene itself.

In his studio, Hartgen does rough studies on small standard drawing pads, using the field sketches for reference, evolving composition and dramatic effects. This develops into the basic picture content and design. Then he allows the sheet to dry, turns it over, soaks it with a sponge, and stretches it over an open frame of pine strapping, using staples around the edge. He is careful not to pull the wet paper too taut, for he knows that it will grow drum-tight as it dries. Properly stretched, the paper will remain perfectly smooth without great waves or surface irregularities.

Hartgen varies his technique according to the subject and theme of his painting. He has never prescribed to the exclusive use of the wet-on-wet, wet-on-dry, or the dry-on-dry approach, since he has always felt these should be dictated by the subject and statement. Some call for a wettish approach, while others demand dry methods. He has even used a wash over some dry brush work, reversing the normal procedure, in order to obtain certain effects. He paints seascapes with broad strokes of crashing waves; forest scenes with fine detail.

Generally, however, he proceeds to lay in large, broad design areas with wide brushes first, working at a quick pace, sometimes skimming the surface lightly to leave a white-paper sparkle. Then he moves to deeper, darker tones and smaller statements, using finer brushes as the work becomes more detailed, finally ending with delicate opaque strokes, using a no. oo brush from which some hairs have been plucked. In this final stage, it is often necessary to put the painting on an easel and work with it in a vertical position to get stand-off perspective.

Since he quite often shows paintings without glass, Hartgen generally mounts the papers (having cut them from the stretcher strips) onto illustration or fine mounting board, using a fine framer's adhesive or a white or rice flour paste. Then the work is allowed to dry for several days, pressed between sheets of flat steel.

W. Emerton Heitland

Wind on the Beach
Watercolor 20" x 24"

I<small>N</small> *Wind on the Beach*, reproduced on the facing page, W. Emerton Heitland used the following palette: alizarin crimson, burnt sienna, Indian yellow, Prussian green, emerald green, Prussian blue, and Payne's gray. He painted with large round brushes which are particularly effective in the arc-like strokes of the palm trees and the ragged shapes of the clouds. The effect of intense sunlight is heightened by the white paper, modified here and there by washes of bright color, and thrown into contrast with the dark foliage behind the figures. Notice that the light is concentrated in the foreground, and that the background forms the darkest element in the picture.

The essence of this watercolor is simplicity of means. The artist obviously painted it with the fewest possible strokes of the brush. Many of the trees are simply a single flat tone and only one tree—the tallest—is painted in any detail; the others are bold silhouettes. In the same way, the figures are essentially flat shapes with dark accents of color for faces, arms, and feet; splashes of transparent shadow contrast with bare paper in the sunlit planes.

The sky is wet-in-wet in some areas and dry in others. For example, the upper right hand corner started out as a wet-in-wet passage. When this was dry, the hard-edged darker shapes were painted in. The artist took advantage of happy accidents in creating the lively cloud shapes in this dramatic sky.

The cadensed movement of the composition is accentuated not only by the tilt of the wind-blown trees and the moving figures, but even by the obliquely placed driftwood in the right foreground. But to keep everything from rushing out of the picture to the right, the weight of the trees and figures is concentrated at the center and left.

Robert Higgs

Lowlands
Watercolor 16½" x 29¼"

Rᴏʙᴇʀᴛ ʜɪɢɢs (1916–1967) ᴅʀᴇᴡ ᴄᴏɴsᴛᴀɴᴛʟʏ in his sketchbook. In these studies he worked out his major compositions, and even the details of the motif, to such an extent that he seldom made the traditional pencil or charcoal draft on his final watercolor sheet, depending instead on a brush drawn lay-in. In fact, Higgs felt that his sketches were so important—not only to a particular watercolor, but for future use and reference in other paintings—that he never destroyed his sketches, even the most fragmentary ones.

Higgs believed in the value of good materials, and used an assortment of brushes: a no. 10 round sable, a 1″ flat watercolor brush, a small bamboo Japanese brush (for his smaller brushes) and, in the larger brushes, a large white bristle sign writer's brush, and 4″ to 6″ housepainter's brushes for flowing clear water over the paper. He used these large brushes for the first lay-in of big color areas. The first thing he did with a brush was to cut the end of the handle at a 45 degree angle and sand it so it was not rough. He used this wooden edge as a scraper, to give texture to a wash passage while it was still damp. He often used a large painting knife to create certain textural effects, sometimes turning it on its edge to produce fine division lines in his wash patterns.

Higgs experimented with all types of paper, from cover paper (used in print-ing) to the best all-rag paper, but he preferred 300 lb rough-surfaced stock. Al-though he admitted to experimenting on various colored papers, his most substantial watercolors were done on the white, heavy weight, rag stock.

Higgs had a simple color palette, consisting of two blues, two browns, two reds, one orange, two yellows, black, and a dark green.

At times he liked to saturate the paper on both sides (when using 140 lb paper), in order to get it very wet. Other times, he dampened one side only. He first brushed larger color patterns on the sheet very quickly, but finally painted in a rather dry manner, taking care not to overwork this part. If he found he was getting involved with too much detail, he placed the painting aside for several days. Only then could he tell whether it needed to be discarded or whether it could be rescued.

When painting *full sheet* watercolors, Higgs always worked from notes and small thumbnail sketches before he began the painting. He made small water-colors quickly, without preliminary sketches, and recommended it as a regular practice for other artists. He liked to start with large shapes first with the larger brushes, and finish with the smaller ones. Some of his best work was attained with the use of only big brushes from start to finish. He believed that a regi-mented manner of working helps artists understand what a big brush can do.

94   Lars Hoftrup

Lars hoftrup (1874–1954) seldom produced a literal transcription of his subject. He selected an attractive motif and then proceeded to arrange it to suit his own ideas of artistic order.

Often he made a brief pencil drawing on a pad before beginning his watercolor. Then only a few guidelines in charcoal or soft pencil were made on the watercolor paper. Next, with a round sable brush charged with lots of water and color, he began his painting. In the early stages, the artist seemed to pay little attention to the form of things. Instead, he swiftly plotted down what appeared to be an abstract arrangement of color pattern. The lightest areas in the composition were left as patches of white paper to be modified later. Hoftrup took great pains, however, to avoid opacity by always mixing his darkest values denser than they appeared in his subject—knowing that the wash would dry lighter in value. In applying his color, the artist did not use a heavy touch, so the wash had a tendency to retain its natural transparency, and to leave tiny specks of white in the depressions of the rough-textured paper. This textural quality may be seen in *Pine City in Green*, reproduced on the facing page, where it contributes life and sparkle to the entire painting.

Lars Hoftrup seldom completed a watercolor in the field. In fact, his pictures appeared about half finished when he packed up his materials and returned to his studio. Here, he placed his watercolor in a mat in a trial frame on an easel, and stood back to study his picture; the creative, concentrated work still went on. Only after due consideration did he take up his painting process; the speed of his outdoor technique was reduced to a snail's pace. When small details were added, color was further qualified by thin washes, and the painting is put back into its frame. Sometimes this process was accomplished the same working day; at other times, it was completed over several days, or even taken up again weeks later. Before applying watercolor additions, Hoftrup frequently used pastel—which is easily removed with a dry cloth and art gum eraser—to change values and color. This process of rigid self-criticism was characteristic of the painter.

Largely self-taught, Hoftrup never stopped experimenting with his techniques and his materials. Although he said he preferred a heavy, rough-textured paper, he painted handsomely on the smoothest stock. His usual watercolor pads were 15″ x 20″, but he seemed equally happy working on a large full sheet, or making miniature sketches. Although one is struck by the quality of his color, his small watercolor box was only an 8″ white dinner plate which served as his unorthodox palette. He used the following colors: yellow ochre, cadmium orange deep, cadmium lemon, burnt sienna, alizarin crimson, ultramarine blue, Prussian blue, viridian green, raw sienna, burnt umber, cadmium red pale, cerulean blue, Payne's gray, and Hooker's green. Two brushes filled his needs: a large round sable and a sign writer's long sable, about no. 11.

Earl Horter

Rainy Night—Chinatown
Watercolor 20" x 22"
Collection, Mrs. Betty Horter

THE COLOR SENSE which Earl Horter (1881-1940) revealed in his painting grew out of his monochromatic predilections: muted and urbane. Almost always on the cool side of the palette, it never threatened to seize the picture. In referring to his work, Horter once said, "I always seem to paint with ice water."

The palette Horter used in this painting is obviously restricted to browns and blues, with a touch of yellow. Brown and blue have been used to mix a surprising range of warm and cool grays, gray-browns, ruddier browns, yellow-browns, blues, and greens. This is an excellent example of how just a few colors can create the illusion of a full color range.

The moldering surfaces of the old buildings have been rendered wet-in-wet with blurs of warm and cool tones flowing into one another in seemingly unpredictable but actually controlled ways. The artist has made particularly good use of the tendency of ultramarine blue and burnt umber—both heavy pigments —to granulate, settling into the valleys of the paper and forming rough mottled passages which give the effect of crumbling masonry. A similar effect appears in the sky, where the brooding darkness is enhanced by this granulation. Notice how a light tone has been scrubbed out around the steeple to accentuate the darkness of this architectural form, the keystone holding this painting together.

This subtle architectural painting is based entirely on a carefully planned geometric design which was obviously thought out carefully beforehand. The picture relies on the interplay of verticals and diagonals and the focus is a light-filled triangle just off-center. The effect is very much like a beautifully lit stage setting in which dark figures are silhouetted against the light. In fact, the artist reverses the expected pattern of light and dark by placing the darker buildings in the foreground and illuminating the building at the end of the street, which then contrasts sharply with the dark silhouette of the church steeple in the distance.

Philip Jamison

WPEN
Watercolor 12½" x 28½"

PHILIP JAMISON'S SUBJECTS are all derived from nature. The things he paints are close to him: the hills that surround his home, the houses among the hills, the flowers that grow nearby, his children. In all these, he sees a beauty that he attempts to capture for himself and for others. In many instances, this may be the less obvious appeal of a neighbor's mailbox or of a snow-trodden clump of weeds. It does not matter whether they have existed for hours, days, or centuries, or whether he is the only one who can see their beauty. Something within them arouses an interest which he believes can be captured and imparted to others. Since he often tries to express the patina of time, an effect which cannot be achieved with a few bold strokes, his paintings tend to be subtle in color and handling. He also favors neutral colors, because they are less tiring to him than bright ones.

Although, at one time, Jamison did all his watercolors outdoors, he now prefers working more in the studio. He is, of course, constantly in the field studying nature for inspiration. During the actual painting, however, the scene seems to be a deterrent to his creativeness. He does not wish to be bound by factual observation, for he paints by feeling and emotion, rather than from the subject. Consequently, although he has a so-called "realistic approach," his finished paintings often bear little resemblance to the sources of his inspiration. He tries, in short, to transfer to paper the way he *feels* about the subject, rather than how it actually looks.

Jamison begins his watercolor with an abstract pattern which is usually simple in design and color. From this point, he starts building with a good bit of enthusiasm and abandon. When possible, he tries to keep the painting in a fluid state so that he can push it around and make revisions. He has developed a method of combining watercolor with charcoal to achieve greater freedom and more subtleties than he can enjoy with watercolor alone.

This combination was used for *WPEN* (reproduced here), a painting of a Philadelphia intersection which he saw every week for some years. Each time he passed the crossing, he was intrigued by the patterns formed by the buildings, poles, and wires. He tried to capture the manner in which all these elements meshed to form a unified design. He also used reflections of the components, and changed colors, values, and composition to enhance his original conception.

*A beauty
difficult to do*

Guatemalan Church Ruins
Watercolor 21½" x 29"
Collection, Mr. and Mrs. Seymour Schwartz

AVERY JOHNSON PAINTS all his watercolors in his studio; these are carefully planned in advance and slowly developed.

First Johnson accumulates the source material. This is mostly in the form of field sketches: line drawings done with a free-flowing fountain pen, with broad, watercolor style tonal passages smudged in with a moistened finger. Details requiring more intricate treatment are recorded separately in pencil. These field drawings often include copious marginal notes covering color and value relationships, and any other pertinent aspects of the subject. Averse to bulky paraphernalia, Johnson carries a stationery-size clip board with a good bond paper.

In his studio, Johnson organizes his painting by drawing a series of pencil thumbnails in which the elements of the proposed painting are arranged primarily as abstract shapes. He may use material from several field sketches. From the most promising of these arrangements, Johnson does a miniature painting at an easily transferable scale, usually 11" x 15" for a 22" x 30" full sheet painting. Here he works out all the color relationships.

Well before reaching this stage, he has decided which of several technical procedures he will use. Usually, the nature of the subject and the colors involved influence this choice, but sometimes it is nothing more profound than what method he would most enjoy at the moment. One of these methods is the combination of waterproof India ink with color washes. The combining of ink and wash is common enough; most artists put the ink on over, or into, washes already on the paper, but Johnson does the ink work first, creating grays. But he is careful not to do a drawing that will compete with the final painting.

Most of the ink work is drawn with reed pens that he cuts from bamboo-like sections of dried pampas grass. They work beautifully on rough paper, don't catch in the grain, give a rough line on dry surfaces, are more versatile than brushes in wet areas, and are clumsy enough to discourage any tendency to fussiness. He frequently uses a jet-pak sprayer, often drawing on a dry surface and giving a quick spray to induce limited creeping effects.

By the time he is ready to paint, the disciplined phase is over and he is free to paint spontaneously. In order for the ink to be an integral part of the painting, the artist uses the most transparent watercolors to prevent the deposit of pigment over the ink—alizarin, phthalocyanine blue and green, burnt sienna, and the like —avoiding such colors as the cadmiums and ultramarine blue. His waterproof ink underpainting remains intact if he has to sponge off areas for color revisions.

Johnson varies his choice of paper depending on what effects he wants to achieve. For most of his large paintings he uses a 300 lb, pure linen, rough, hand-made, hard paper, which is non-yellowing. For line and wash drawings in ink, he uses a soft, tan, medium-rough paper that does not darken with age.

Cecile Johnson

Taiwan
Watercolor 15" x 30"
Collection, U.S. Navy

Bᴇᴄᴀᴜꜱᴇ ꜱʜᴇ ʙᴇʟɪᴇᴠᴇꜱ that the initial painting surface in a watercolor is extremely important, Cecile Johnson tries to have a variety of papers on hand. She usually uses a 300 lb sheet or a mounted board. For sketching, the artist uses a Whatman board (no longer available) and nos. 5 and 8 sable rounds, which she dips into black and sienna inks. When traveling, an India ink drawing pen and felt-tip pens are more practical for sketching, the large felt nib for masses and the fine pen line for detail. Thus, she has no trouble with leaky caps or tops due to changes in altitude. For painting, the artist uses a 2″ brush as well as a no. 12 or no. 13 round sable; stubby 1″ flat, a long-haired flat, and a rigger.

Aside from the usual colors found on many palettes (cadmium yellow, cadmium orange, yellow ochre, vermilion or cadmium red, raw sienna, burnt sienna, alizarin crimson, cerulean blue, ultramarine, cobalt blue, Prussian or phthalocyanine green, burnt umber, Payne's gray, ivory black), she occasionally adds aureolin yellow, Indian red, and warm sepia. She does not use all of these in any one painting.

Taiwan was painted in Tsoying, Formosa. Here, as in other crowded places in the Orient, she felt that blocking in colors first and reinforcing them later with brush and ink line was a solution for the many details and complexities of the scene. Thus, she could catch the activity as it occurred. Her style always suits the subject. For example, when painting the great sky masses of luminous clouds shouldered by Mount Kilimanjaro, she would not use a calligraphic style, but would apply wet-into-wet washes, using wide brushes and rich colors. When painting the Inland Sea in Japan, she instinctively would use the simple graded washes, close values, and tracery trees of the Japanese style.

a favorite
for simplicity and color

Norman Kent

The Hannoch House
Watercolor 11½" x 15½"
Collection, J. D. Young

WHILE PAINTING A FULL SHEET (22" x 30") is often regarded as the ultimate in watercolor facility, it is only fair to state that there are numerous examples of even larger ones (the work of Charles Burchfield is a case in point) and there are innumerable painters—from the English masters of the early nineteenth century, down to artists of all schools in the present—who have preferred to work in smaller scale, especially those who paint outdoors.

The present artist is one such watercolorist, and though the example reproduced is approximately only a quarter sheet (he more often paints on half sheets), the character of its freely painted forms is the result of his respect for transient light effects recorded spontaneously.

Except for a few very minor adjustments in color and values made in the studio, this small watercolor exhibits the broad pattern of its rapid execution.

The pencil draft that preceded the first application of color was only skeletal—concerned with the placement of the house, the flanking trees, the river vista, and the design of the foreground. This took about ten minutes, but it *followed* a half hour of considering various positions and, having settled on this view, of sitting down (on a folding stool) and studying every aspect of its lighting, its coloration, and its spatial arrangement.

The actual painting was done with a no. 12 sable brush on a block of 140 lb, medium rough, imported paper. The color palette consisted of alizarin crimson, vermilion, lemon yellow, cadmium yellow, Hooker's green, cobalt, ultramarine, cerulean and Prussian blues, burnt umber, burnt sienna, and Payne's gray.

Since the key to this watercolor was the shadowed end of this old plastered house, all other values were related to it. Although the sun was warm on this September day, the atmosphere was cool in the late afternoon light. Surrounding a few patches of sunlit earth and little accents of red in the brick foundation, all else was a study in ranges from blue to blue-green, green to green-yellow, purple-blue to red-purple.

After the main masses of color had been blocked in, special attention was given to the dark accents of tree trunks and limbs, the cast shadows across the left foreground and their flickering pattern on the roof. For a final touch of necessary warmth, a light pink was added to the facade and sky.

The whole painting process was completed in about one half hour, but consistent with a practice learned years ago, before the artist could decide the success or failure of his painting, he waited until he had arrived home to see his watercolor in indoor light, supported by a trial mat covered by a sheet of glass. This is more important to the artist than its appearance on the spot, where a combination of strong light and tired eyes dull the ability to judge the quality of any watercolor.

Alfred Khouri

Summer Bouquet
Watercolor 22" x 17"

Alfred khouri (1915-1962) felt that the finest materials are essential to paint a watercolor. He used an 18" x 24" Masonite board faced on one side with white enamel (any smooth, rigid board will do) as a support for 140 lb rough rag paper. Two sponges—a large rectangular cellulose kitchen sponge, and a smaller one such as that used by photographers to wipe off negatives after washing—were an important part of his equipment. His three brushes were nos. 8 and 10 round sable, and a flat 1" sable with a plastic handle which was beveled at one end. He liked a lot of mixing area, so he used a flat 16" x 20" white enameled palette that was made for an oil painting set. Two coffee cans served as convenient containers for water.

Rather than cut his paper down to the desired size, Khouri always tore it by creasing it a few times and tore it to preserve the deckled-edge effect. Then the finished painting could be mounted on mat board or matted in the conventional way, depending on the effect he wanted.

Khouri painted *Summer Bouquet* (reproduced on the facing page) as a two-hour demonstration of the wet-in-wet technique. With a 2H pencil, Khouri drew the pitcher of flowers loosely. Then he applied water generously to both sides of the paper, using a sponge.

While the paper was absorbing the water, he squeezed out generous amounts of color on the top edge of his palette in this sequence: Naples yellow, cadmium yellow lemon, cadmium yellow medium, cadmium orange, vermilion light, cadmium red light, cadmium red deep, yellow ochre, raw sienna, raw umber, and sepia natural. On the left hand edge he placed alizarin crimson golden, cerulean blue, cobalt blue, French ultramarine blue, phthalocyanine blue, sap green, Hooker's green deep, viridian, phthalocyanine green, ivory black, and permanent mauve.

From the limp, saturated paper, Khouri poured off the excess water and placed the paper in a horizontal position. He loosely applied a soupy mixture of colors for the background, moving his sable from the top down. The wet paper ran the colors together in a free wash. Where necessary, Khouri used the small sponge to lift the color away to keep the flower area clean white.

To suggest a flat plane, he applied the foreground colors with a sponge, merely suggesting the pitcher. Khouri floated in the color for each bloom as lightly as possible, using the sponge again in areas where the paint was running too freely. Next he painted in the foliage masses, with care to avoid the flower areas. As the paper dried more and more, Khouri attended to the details. He used the beveled tip of his brush handle to press out some of the still-moist green color to highlight and suggest some of the stems and veins in the foliage area. With the no. 8 round sable, he drew in some of the petal and leaf shapes. By the time the paper was nearly dry, he had developed the other details and added accents.

After deciding that columbus circle was the subject he was looking for, Dong Kingman proceeded to do a very rough pencil sketch. He then went back to his studio and studied it in a number of brush sketches, coming to the conclusion that it would be a good thing to develop. He returned to the spot and started working, using his sketch pad, and working in brush line with very light watercolor of no particular shade. He lowered the buildings so the monument would rise against the dark sky, since he felt it was very beautiful this way. He also changed the buildings to suit the composition he had previously developed in his studio studies, until he got exactly what he wanted. He then put aside the sketch pad, got out his watercolor paper and in very light brush lines copied what he had produced on the sketch pad.

Now he had to work in his values, and so Kingman laid a light wash of color on the picture to indicate the strong values, and then waited for it to dry. Now he had a rough idea of his dark and light values, so he began with the color, trying to make it as powerful as the dark should be, and as light as it should be, concentrating on the picture as a whole. After he had painted the monument and the street lights, a few people here and there, some of the buildings, and the background, he proceeded to lay in the sky, after which he worked, in detail, the rest of the picture. What caught his eye were the startling accents of sunlit planes contrasting with darkening clouds, splashes of brilliant color intermingled with tonal grays, stabs of dark accents, the sweep of the whole colorful mass against a windy sky. He had not yet put the shadow in when a few drops of rain came, causing him to go back to his studio, which was just as well because many of his pictures are completed indoors anyhow.

Contrary to the somewhat general practice, Kingman usually leaves the sky of his painting until almost the last. He feels that in so doing he can better adjust this vital factor in the all-over effect of the picture.

Kingman's color is strong, varied, and clean; it is hard to believe that the result can come out of his tiny paint box lying on the pavement at his feet. All the water he requires is carried in the rectangular receptacle standing at one end of the palette. It holds barely a half pint. He uses no paint cloth for cleaning his two brushes which he makes do all the work.

Robert H. Laessig

Sunflowers
Watercolor 35¾" x 50"
Collection, Dr. and Mrs. Loren Eiseley

Bold, stark sunflowers and delicate milkweed pods are subject matter to which Robert H. Laessig returns again and again because they embody the two elements which concern him most in painting: the sunflower became a favorite after a search for something of beauty which would combine large masses with decorative detail. The artist enjoys arranging foliage and grasses for painting. During summer and fall, he takes many color slides and gathers dried grasses in order to have a backlog of subject matter for the winter months. Nature is a never-ending source of material, and all too little time is spent on-the-spot sketching and painting. Sketching from nature should never be neglected for long, Laessig says.

Because he emphasizes draughtsmanship in his work, Laessig spends considerable time in drawing most of his subjects. With a sharp pencil, he often begins the underpinning of his watercolor by carefully delineating the subject. At times this drawing may control the painting, or it may merely be the skeleton that peeps through here and there to give structure to the work. He does numerous paintings on a non-woven rayon material similar to Japanese paper. Too much erasing can make holes in the surface of this fabric, so the original sketch must be fairly sure, a procedure that requires patience and discipline. Even though the artist starts with a fine drawing, there are many details he develops during the course of his painting, and therefore he does not make many small roughs. The absorbent cloth holds the water very well, permitting experiments with different hues without the paint running and distorting forms. Its absorbent character (it remains wet for a long time) allows ample time to paint around light areas.

Before starting to paint, Laessig frequently spatters light shades of casein over the cloth to produce many unusual effects. Very often, after laying in the masses and detail over the basic drawing, the watercolor appears too brittle and disciplined. By turning it over, he may find that charming areas of color had bled through, so he may redevelop the painting on this reverse side. This necessitates extra work, but the final effect is often worth the effort.

PRACTICALLY ALL OF BORIS LEVEN'S WATERCOLORS are painted from nature. On most occasions, the subject matter is an old friend—a "spot" which he has seen a number of times and has stored away in his memory for timely use. Occasionally, he turns to new "spots" to capture new effects and fresh illusions.

With a few pencil lines, Leven blocks out the major elements of the composition. He keeps the color quite wet and the whole picture moving right from the start until it is built up to a desired degree. Details and points of emphasis are strengthened after the entire picture takes its proper form. Generally, he works very fast and, as a rule, the sketch is completed on the spot.

Leven prefers to use tube colors and his palette consists of ivory black, permanent blue, alizarin crimson, burnt sienna, yellow ochre, gamboge. Since brushes are of great importance, he uses the best Winsor & Newton sable brushes in no. 12 and no. 8. In paper, he prefers medium rough texture, using sheets approximately 16″ x 24″. But he has painted on all kinds of textures with all kinds of colors and brushes. (He painted *Paris, Rue St. Louis*, which is reproduced here, on fairly smooth illustration board, capitalizing on the transparency of his direct washes.) From these experiments, Leven believes he has gained the knowledge which has helped him to better understand the medium and to use it with greater intelligence and imagination.

Since watercolor is flexible, reasonably easy to handle, direct, and requires such simple equipment, Leven believes it is the ideal medium for sketching. Using watercolor, one can register one's thoughts, capture an impression with speed and accuracy. He feels its characteristics offer endless possibilities.

Referring to the novice, Leven said, "The beginner will see, once there is an inspiration of something to say, that he will find a way to communicate his thoughts and ideals. It might be difficult at first. With practice, however, he will discover many new ways, new methods, and techniques. His language will become more crisp, direct, and to the point."

114   Joseph Margulies

JOSEPH MARGULIES KEEPS his palette simple, with six brilliant transparent colors from top quality manufacturers. From left to right on his palette, he places French ultramarine blue, alizarin crimson, cadmium red light or vermilion, cadmium orange, cadmium lemon yellow, and cerulean blue. Sometimes he adds viridian green, but only rarely. He feels that he can obtain the earth colors—the siennas, umbers, and ochres, and various greens, violets, and grays—from a mixture of the above colors with far better harmony and control than from ready-made ones. Naturally, it requires much experimentation with this simple palette to see what endless variety of hues can be achieved before delving headlong into portraiture.

Margulies uses two sable pointed brushes (nos. 6 and 12), two flat sables (½" and 1") and, for certain effects, a small oil bristle brush. He uses a 300 lb semi-rough, all-rag paper. The artist feels that it is false economy to use any but the finest brushes, paint, and paper.

Although there are many ways to paint a watercolor portrait, Margulies explained his general method employed for the portrait of the late Dean Cornwell, reproduced here. After directing his model to a chair on the model stand, Margulies placed his light sketching easel about six feet away and tilted the board with his sheet of paper to a forty-five degree angle. Then he drew in pencil for about five minutes to determine the general composition and placement of the head and shoulders. Next he used water and the largest brush to saturate the whole head area and he mixed a flesh tint to wash in the lightest passages. Gradually, he modeled with less water and more color, adding form and drawing as he worked. He blocked in only the general features.

After a short rest, Margulies began the last important phase of the portrait. He worked over the entire surface with short accents of color and tone to bring the features into sharper focus, while at the same time interpreting and expressing his model as he saw him. For some smaller areas like the eyes, mouth, and glasses, he worked carefully, using small sable and oil brushes—sometimes with almost a dry brush and then again with plenty of water and little paint. Finally, only a few major accents remained and, with a likeness achieved, these were added with confidence. The sketch portrait was complete.

Ordinarily, Margulies prefers at least two sittings for a watercolor portrait, but in this instance he was obliged to concentrate his working time into one session.

This is excellent
Darks, lights, figures

When roy mason begins to paint—which he prefers to do outdoors—he first makes preliminary watercolor sketches in quarter scale (approximately 11" x 15") which will later become full sheet (22" x 30") paintings. Here he pays particular attention to the design of the three simple values—the lightest light, the middle tone, and the darkest dark—by reducing the forms of his subject to these large patterns. If a human figure or wild life are to be part of the final picture, he tries to place them in the initial sketch. For him, these will belong more completely to their surroundings if they are conceived in this early stage, though he does not hesitate to add or omit figures on the full sheet when it serves his purpose.

Mason thoughtfully studies his sketches for improvement in color and design. After he has selected one, he squares it up and enlarges it to the final sheet, drawing freehand with charcoal. When this linear draft is completed, he dusts it down to a faint image. Then he plans his attack: the parts he will finish first, the range of values, the accenting of minor details, all the mechanics of producing the finished job. From this point, he paints directly, flowing on the washes with as pure a color mixture as he can manage.

Mason uses the best materials available. In the field, he works on a watercolor easel, and frequently resorts to a large, green garden umbrella to protect his eyes from undue strain. In his studio, he works at a tilt-top table, but leaves the paper unfixed so that he can move it freely to control the washes. He has used a variety of heavy weight handmade papers, but he prefers an English brand, rough surface, in 400 lb weight. After selecting a sheet and inspecting it for flaws (even the best sometimes has foreign "nubbins" on its surface), he sponges it thoroughly on both sides with clean, cold water. Then he dries the sheet under mild pressure so that it will lie flat as a board.

The artist's brushes are different from those used by most watercolorists, because he employs both the sable and the bristle. The red sables are no. 8; two riggers, nos. 6 and 10; and a very large flat wash brush. The bristles are a Fitch no. 2 and a ½" brush shaved to a sharp chisel edge.

His usual palette consists of top-quality colors: alizarin crimson, orange, raw sienna, raw umber, burnt sienna, sepia, cerulean blue, cobalt blue, French ultramarine blue, Winsor green, Hooker's green no. 2, cadmium yellow pale, yellow ochre, Payne's gray, charcoal gray, Davy's gray, and ivory black.

In addition to the usual tools, Mason makes constant use of cleansing tissue, not only to wipe his brushes, but to mop up certain areas, to soften edges, and to open up lights in dark washes. The great absorbency of this tissue and the fact that it is easier to control than a sponge makes it an ideal tool for the watercolorist. He also uses a small electric hand-blower to dry large washes in the studio.

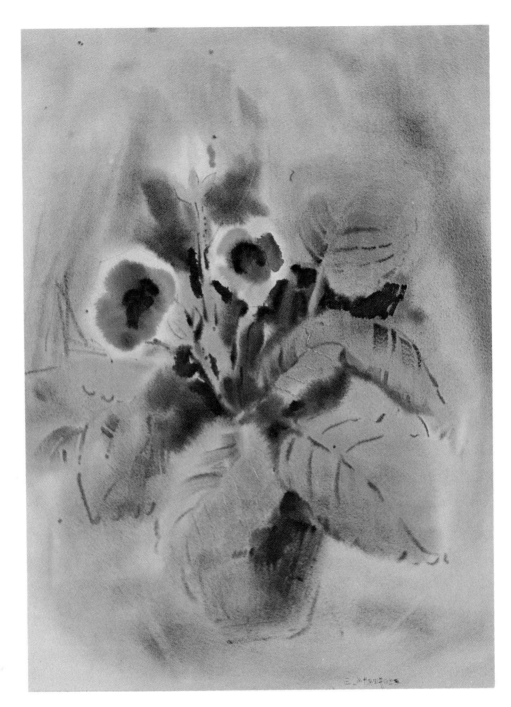

I like the ptg
starts with dark color

118   E. Ingersoll Maurice

Gloxinia
Watercolor 22" x 16"
Collection, Mrs. J. L. Dupré

E. INGERSOLL MAURICE USED a wet-in-wet technique in *Gloxinia*, as in all her flower paintings. Keeping the paper saturated throughout the painting process gives the soft, velvety look she likes to maintain in her flower subjects at all times. (She does not employ the wet technique with landscapes, where she prefers a sharper contrast and more definite shapes.)

The artist generally paints directly, using no preliminary sketches, and barely even looking at the flowers themselves. In fact, she feels the less she sees, the better, and she merely uses the flowers as reference. If her painting seems to demand it, she may make an initial drawing in India ink. This is simply to define a leaf or to accent a blossom and to achieve a variety of line and texture in the composition.

Maurice uses good quality rag paper, about 140 lb; a wide flat, and a couple of letter brushes in different sizes; a quill brush and a bamboo pen which she makes herself out of a cane brake; a wooden spatula (the kind doctors use) for scratching out highlights; a dull penknife; plenty of tissues; and a large sponge. Her palette is round and arranged in the colors of the spectrum, from cadmium yellow through deep red, alizarin crimson, black, Payne's gray, permanent blue, Prussian blue, emerald green, phthalocyanine green, occasionally cobalt violet. She does not use earth colors. She never cleans her palette because she finds a dirty palette keeps the color soft, an effect she wants unless she intentionally paints a bright red or yellow flower.

She wets her paper with a sponge on both sides. This keeps it from warping so that it can lie completely flat on her metal table. Once the paper stops shining from the water, she is ready to paint. First, with her wide brush heavy with paint but otherwise quite dry, she washes in the background. Eliminating the white background immediately gives her great confidence to proceed rapidly. After the background is washed in, she is very careful to protect the silhouette and negative spaces. Working very fast, she then washes in the local color in broad abstract forms. Since she makes no preliminary drawing, she must carefully place her colors in the right areas. As the paper dries, she works in the details, drawing with her brush where necessary. She paints in her darkest darks, using alizarin crimson and phthalocyanine green to get a strong accent that remains very dark even after it dries on the paper.

If she is working into a color—which she tries to avoid—she keeps her brush practically dry so that she won't get a backwash. (In the right places, however, she finds backwashes very satisfying.) To deepen the colors, which is sometimes absolutely necessary, she waits until the paper is dry, then wets a large area with a clean brush and drops the color into it, being careful not to bring it all the way to the edge, especially in a large space. This procedure prevents the area from looking as if it has been corrected.

Fred L. Messersmith

Shrimp Boats, New Smyrna
Casein 19⅝" x 28"
Collection, Henry Rossell

AFTER PAINTING for a number of years on heavy, all-rag paper in a traditional technique, Fred Messersmith became interested in the possibilities of working on Japanese rice paper with casein. He selected rice paper after seeing some of the exciting work of Morris Graves, and after long study of Oriental art. This paper has a highly absorbent, translucent quality, and manages to retain brilliant color even after repeated soakings. Though fragility does pose some problems in handling, these can be solved with a healthy respect for the limitations of rice paper as a painting surface—and careful handling before, during, and after painting. The paper is practically impossible to stretch before painting, so Messersmith finds it desirable to work on a flat table with a layer of newsprint beneath the rice paper to absorb the excess moisture.

The artist uses full sheets of Sekishu white, 24" x 39", and always has a double-thick mat cut for a frame. The minute the painting is finished, he fastens the rice paper securely to the mat on all sides with 1" masking tape. As it dries, it stretches wrinkle-free and drum-tight. He then frames the picture behind glass.

The artist uses casein because of its flexibility, compared to transparent watercolor. In a single stroke, one can manipulate the paint from a thin wash to opaqueness. He also discovered that an extremely exciting calligraphic line may be obtained by diluting a color and letting it flow from the edge of his painting knife. When he applies color, Messersmith never pre-draws his idea on the rice paper. Instead, he places his sketch in clear view and relies upon his ability to coordinate hand and eye at the right moment.

Messersmith wets the paper all over with the sponge and works from the top down, applying sky washes with a large 3" brush. In fact, he tries to use the largest brush possible as long as he can. As the subject comes into focus, he swings to an opaque technique with the knife. Finally, he adds "calligraphy" with the painting knife, being careful always to drag its edge without puncturing the paper. This method, not being conducive to work in the field, means that Messersmith paints from sketches—made with a 4B pencil—or from snapshots.

His other materials are few and simple. In addition to the table, newsprint, masking tape, and mat, he uses an old white china platter for mixing color; a Celotex sponge for wetting the paper or for applying broad washes; a painting knife worn paper-thin from years of use; and the following brushes: a no. 20 flat bristle brush, a no. 5 Chinese brush, and a small red sable for detail. His palette consists of casein titanium white, ivory black, phthalocyanine green, Naples yellow, cadmium yellow medium, yellow ochre, raw sienna, burnt sienna, raw umber, burnt umber, cadmium red extra-scarlet, and cadmium red deep. He uses this fairly complete palette at the outset, for he feels it is better to have the colors available than to find them lacking at a crucial moment.

Carl N. Molno

Captain Jack
Watercolor and Ink 21" x 29"

BY ABSTRACTING NATURE'S SHAPES—avoiding a factual report—Carl Molno feels he makes a better design statement. He works fast in order not to diminish the initial excitement he finds in the subject matter. Although he makes preliminary sketches, he prefers to improvise on the paper. Consequently, his sketches are not detailed; they are simply a rough rendering of the patterns. He feels that a sketch, if too carefully drawn, creates tension in the artist while he is painting; therefore, he uses his studies merely as gropings for pictorial ideas.

In *Captain Jack*, for example, Molno made thumbnail sketches but discarded them when he started to paint. He drew in the figure first with a black felt-tip marker (non-smearing), then painted with washes of yellow and oranges; next, he painted the buildings in blues and greens; then, wetting the paper, he laid in the sky; and finished up with the boats and water. The final touches of calligraphic lines were also made with a felt-tip marker. After studying the painting, he found that the *first* sky was uninteresting, having neither direction nor gradation. So he rewet the entire area and laid in a new, more dramatic sky.

His palette contains the usual combination of warm and cool tube colors, which he mixes intuitively, since he favors no formal system. His brushes are largely flat ox hair, augmented by round sables, and several sizes of riggers which he uses calligraphically. He paints on both cold pressed and rough paper, handmade, 100% rag, in 140 lb and 300 lb weights.

Molno prefers the wet-in-wet method of watercolor painting, and he does not stretch or mount his paper, since he finds that the 300 lb paper does not require stretching, and the 140 lb—when properly saturated—lies flat. He works wet in the underpainting; then, when the paper is bone dry, he imposes finishing washes and line.

124 Eileen Monaghan

Eileen monaghan (Mrs. Frederic Whitaker) varies her techniques with the specific painting. On one she may use straight watercolor, on another acrylic paints (which she usually treats in the regular transparent watercolor manner), or she may first make a complete black ink drawing with a felt-nib pen and then paint over it with color.

The artist now works mostly in the studio, although she gets most of her inspiration from nature. She becomes fascinated with a single theme—one or more horses, cows, birds, human figures—and builds a composition around the theme. If the subject is a farm animal, she studies it from all angles, follows it about the field, makes sketches, takes photographs. In the studio she draws or paints the model in a small size and changes it around until she has the desired form and character.

Usually, her subject suggests rhythm, a swirl, or a direction which she accepts and tries to follow. She develops the pattern with abstract masses, and then decides where the boundary lines are to be in relation to the subject (which is much easier than fitting the subject to the paper). Sometimes she works in the reverse manner, first making a small abstraction in either black and white or in color, and later converting the meaningless forms into recognizable things she thinks they suggest. In either case, with the composition accepted, she then works out the same pattern on her large sheet. As she proceeds, the abstract background shapes are sometimes—but not always—converted into realistic details.

Her method of applying the paint calls for much brushing, a great deal of swabbing out and repainting. Usually she works with a brush in one hand and a sponge in the other, and the two hands seem to be equally busy. Naturally, all this rubbing and scrubbing calls for a sturdy paper. The only ones that can take the punishment are those with a very hard surface in 300 or 400 lb weight. She prefers the English-made papers. A month or more may elapse between the start and finish of a picture, for she may have as many as a half dozen in process, which she looks at each day and works over again and again as improvements suggest themselves.

Tom Nicholas

Avenue A, Albany
Watercolor 21¾" x 29"
Collection, Roy M. Mason

Tom NICHOLAS MAINTAINS that drawing is the most important factor in the success of a watercolor painting. He feels that an artist should never shy away from a subject because of the problems he may have to solve graphically. For this reason, Nicholas tries to draw as often as possible. Painting from nature, like drawing, is also vital to Nicholas. This does not mean that he copies nature literally, but rather he uses it as a basis from which he gains his own interpretations and conclusions.

The procedure Nicholas uses in painting varies with the subject matter. Although he paints continuously, the time spent painting cannot compare to the amount of time he spends studying each subject in progress as a means of finding his own direction. He begins by making small sketches, usually 7" x 10", in color or black and white. They are treated as broadly as possible. If details are important, he makes several drawings to augment his color sketches. Later, in his studio, he explores the design possibilities of his sketches and makes tonal and color adjustments for the finished painting. He finds that his final paintings are more resolved and the subjects themselves more fully explored when he takes time for preliminary drawing.

Nicholas favors 300lb, medium rough, all-rag paper. After wetting it thoroughly on both sides, he tacks this sheet to a large drawing board. When the paper has completely dried, the artist draws the subject in Davy's gray with a small, pointed, red sable brush. From this stage, avoiding any tricks or flashy effects, his primary concern is the over-all feel or mood of the subject. He finds that tacking a mat over the painting from time to time helps him see his progress more clearly.

Regarding opaque whites, Nicholas maintains that the final results are more important than the means. He does not approve of the use of white as a corrective aid, but if it will create passages obtainable in no other way, he feels its use is valid. To him, there are so many other, more important considerations.

The artist's standard palette is cadmium yellow, yellow ochre, raw sienna, cadmium red, alizarin crimson, burnt sienna, burnt umber, cerulean blue, cobalt blue, ultramarine blue, Winsor blue, Hooker's green, emerald green, Davy's gray, ivory black, and tempera white. Of course, at times only a few of these are incorporated in a single painting. His brushes are all red sable of the finest quality and the ones he uses most frequently are nos. 4, 8, and 12 round, and 1" and 2" sign painter's flats.

A beauty

128   Eliot O'Hara

Eliot o'hara paints fast. He likes to complete a watercolor in a half hour, but seldom takes more than three quarters of an hour. "Your greatest enthusiasm," he will tell you, "is felt during those vital moments of your first attack. And your brush will respond accordingly."

O'Hara uses a big flat varnish brush—2″ wide—a good deal of the time. A few strokes with it will cover a considerable area of sky and water in his picture. He also uses 1″ and ½″ flat sables; a no. 12 round sable; a no. 5 sable, a long-haired sable, and a rigger. He may drag these brushes over the picture with the full length of hair lying on the paper, then in an almost vertical position; or stroking with the thin edge or touching with just a corner. To hasten the painting, O'Hara sometimes attaches two brushes to a single handle.

A list of O'Hara's tools would be incomplete without mention of his fingers. They do some things for him better than brushes. In painting a tree, for example, he will brush in a foliage mass then, with a fingernail, dip into the drip of the wash which has settled in a puddle and lead it down to form small branches connecting foliage with trunk or larger branches.

Occasionally, O'Hara has need for a razor blade. If—as sometimes happens with every painter—he has inadvertently covered up an important white accent, he will outline that spot with a razor blade and peel off the top layer of paper, laying bare the clean paper underneath.

The compartments in O'Hara's 6″ x 9″ palette are well filled with colors: cadmium scarlet, alizarin orange, cadmium yellow deep, cadmium yellow pale, lemon yellow, viridian, monastral blue, cobalt blue, ultramarine blue, alizarin crimson, constitute most of the colors and indicate his preference for the primaries. He does not clean his palette after painting; in fact, some of the color on it may have been squeezed from the tube weeks earlier. During a painting season, the paint does not dry hard from day to day, and even after an interim of several weeks, it is only necessary to wet them when he is about ready for work.

O'Hara employs water sparingly. He uses the minimum amount of water required to float the pigment in a wash and does a great deal of mixing actually on the painting itself. He never has an excess left in his palette. To know that a pint jar of water serves for an entire painting gives more than a hint of his method of handling color.

Generally, O'Hara paints on a four-ply medium surface paper or a smooth surface illustration board. This is heavy enough not to buckle and so does not require stretching. The two chief advantages of a smooth paper, according to O'Hara, are the subtleties or the brilliance of the colors shown on it. The chief reason for this is that the light falls on a framed or matted picture either from the top or from one side. With a rough-grained paper each lump, therefore, has a lighted side and a shaded side and sometimes even a cast shadow, causing one to often see the paper more than the colors.

Rudolph Ohrning

Shadows
Watercolor 20" x 14½"
Collection, Jerry Ferm

R UDOLPH OHRNING FINDS many motifs in the city—he lives in a suburb of Chicago —and in areas outside the metropolis. In selecting a subject, he tries to be aware not only of the major attraction, but of everything that surrounds it. If he cannot sketch or paint directly on location, he records the subject with the aid of the camera, without being enslaved by the subsequent print. He usually completes his paintings in his studio, since he is more relaxed by the convenience of having all his materials at hand.

Ohrning's favorite papers are handmade, of rough texture, in a medium weight. He usually stretches the paper by immersing it in water for several minutes, and after letting the excess water drip off, he then mounts it on a ⅛" plywood board, with brown paper tape 3" wide. This combination must be allowed to dry completely before any painting is done on it.

With the exception of some very large-sized ox hair brushes, used for preliminary washes, his favorites include nos. 11, 8, and 6 round sables, along with some wide, flat ones.

Ohrning's colors include lemon yellow, cadmium yellow pale, yellow ochre, cadmium orange, vermilion, alizarin crimson, Indian red, burnt sienna, burnt umber, sepia, cobalt blue, cerulean blue, phthalocyanine blue and green, Hooker's green dark, sap green, Prussian blue, and Payne's gray. He mixes his colors on a white enameled butcher's tray.

Ohrning sketches his subject in pencil first before starting to paint. A landscape needs very little preliminary drawing, while an architectural subject requires considerably more framework. His method of painting is a combination of very wet passages with some dry-brush applications. He usually goes over much of the painting in a loose manner, trying to establish color balance and values, later accenting the detail with dry-brush to solidify areas of the composition.

Excellent but Salorious

J. Olaf Olson

Boatyard at Noank
Watercolor 16½" x 23"

Bᴇᴄᴀᴜꜱᴇ ʜᴇ ʙᴇʟɪᴇᴠᴇꜱ that working on location produces greater spontaneity and retains the freshness of color and light in watercolor, J. Olaf Olson paints directly from nature. Although he frequently adds work on his paintings in the studio, the major patterns are produced on the spot. To him, the great challenge of watercolor is choosing colors and values, deciding on harmonies and contrasts, putting down a concentration of ideas, and creating from these elements an integrated whole—all in one sitting.

Olson carefully works out the drawing before he begins to paint. This allows him to concentrate on the problems of washes, color, and values, and gives him greater freedom while dealing with the crucial aspects of his motif.

Watercolor is a convenient medium for working out-of-doors since the necessary equipment can be easily transported. However, weather conditions often produce widely variable lighting effects in a short period of time and these can lead to technical complications. For this reason, Olson first establishes those elements in the subject which will change most with the shift in the sun's position, or with changes in tide or wind.

Since the sky is the key to the overall atmosphere of a landscape, Olson freely composes the patterns of clouds and light—rather than painting precisely the sky before him—as a means of gaining greater expression. There are certain drawbacks to this method, but he advises this course to avoid the frustration of an imitative background.

The artist works directly on dry paper with the sheet being set at a fairly steep angle, and uses only transparent watercolors of the best quality. He feels it is important to develop the ability to estimate color values on the *palette*, rather than on the paper. Paintings in watercolor are best served when the colors are strong and values have a wide range. In his opinion, it is not the best medium for painting a subject with predominantly low-keyed or close-valued elements.

In *Boatyard at Noank*, he tried to gain sufficiently strong contrasts throughout in order to give greater interest to the whiteness of the boat and to provide interest in the texture of the surfaces. The sky was freely composed to give a turbulent quality, and to keep its values dark enough not to conflict with those of the boat. The details in the foreground were calculated to cause the eye to move easily into the composition.

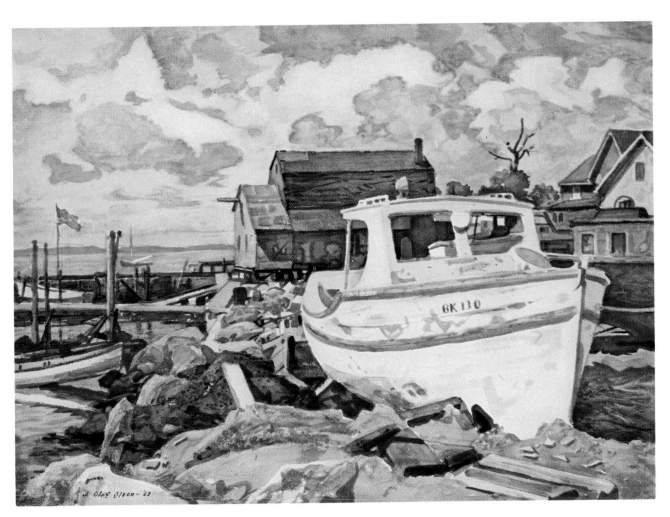

134   Gerry Peirce

COLOR, TO GERRY PEIRCE, is a sensation and not a measurable factor in scientific terms; it is light. His palette, therefore, is set out in relation to light expressed through color. It is arranged in spectrum sequence with one side for brilliants and the other for low-intensity colors. On the bright side are three staining transparent primaries: new gamboge, monastral blue, and alizarin crimson. To this he adds monastral green as a transparent member in the secondary family. On the low-intensity side are brown madder and indigo. New gamboge, even though brilliant, completes the triad. As needed, he adds the cadmium yellows, oranges and reds, earth colors, and occasionally the Mars group. His attempt in painting is to keep both light and dark passages as clean and resilient as possible, utilizing to the fullest the luminosity of white paper to achieve a feeling of light. This is best accomplished through transparent color. His materials must be the best, for he cannot interpret light through inferior paint or dull papers.

When working outside, Peirce is more comfortable standing at a table. The one he uses is light and has a second top hinged to one side so that it can be lifted to shade the paper. The surface is large enough for a white plastic palette, two water containers (ice bags in his case), and miscellaneous brushes.

Landscape has always been his first interest, because he regards nature as a source from which great life principles can be observed and proven. Suppose he is painting a mountain. He starts first by making himself as comfortable as possible. He will forget the mountain as his subject, but will think of it instead as a bed of silt once building in the bottom of an ancient sea—an island in the ocean. He will feel it in relation to the limitless rhythm of the clouds and surging growth of earth. When he has relaxed enough to be aware of the oneness of all things and is ready to paint, through that painting should come an expression of significance about the mountain. Technical procedures will, of course, be governed by what he wants to express.

Technical procedures in the studio are similar to those in the field, made easier possibly by more comfortable working conditions and more materials. Here he finds it interesting to experiment with new approaches to painting that will add significance to expression. He is not a great believer in styles, but when it is necessary to paint inside, it is also often necessary to do a watercolor over in many different ways until he achieves a painting that satisfies him completely.

C. Robert Perrin

Nantucket Narrative
Watercolor 25" x 21"
Collection, Mr. and Mrs. Robert L. Cohen

IN HIS PAINTING, C. Robert Perrin follows four simple stages: first, he sketches the subject as simply and as rapidly as he can; then he covers the entire paper with the local color of all objects as they appear in sunlight; textures are next; and lastly he introduces the shadows, details, and dark accents. This means a progression from light to dark, from distance to foreground. Of course, there are exceptions to every rule and he maintains that he breaks them all, at times.

Perrin feels that a crisp and well-rendered watercolor should not take more than two and a half hours to complete. Good timing, he states, is required in watercolor painting: knowing when to apply the second wash, when to bleed colors, when to use a dry brush.

Perrin paints, standing or sitting, with the paper tilted, and he holds his brushes at arm's length by the tip of the handle to achieve complete freedom. Any brush capable of doing the job at hand is the brush he will use, and he has all kinds: from Japanese brushes with bristles 3" long, to stripers, varnish brushes, and the conventional round and flat sables. Other aids include glycerin (which retards drying and alters paint consistency), an artesian-well palette, masking liquid, and a palette knife. His colors consist of sepia, Payne's gray, burnt sienna, burnt umber, alizarin crimson, vermilion, yellow ochre, lemon yellow, cadmium yellow, brown madder (alizarin), French ultramarine, viridian, and Hooker's green dark.

To Perrin, there is no greater joy than getting out and doing on-the-spot watercolors. He has found a remedy to the frustrating problem of the parked car obstructing his view while he is midway in a painting. His first solution was to paint standing on a platform that he built on top of his car. Later he acquired what he calls "a studio on wheels": a Volkswagen Microbus. His platform consists of heavy plywood with two detachable aluminum legs which he rests on the rear of the front seat. He opens the roof, stands on the platform, and gets a good elevated view of his subject.

Excellent
beautifull color

138 John Pike

Winter Evening
Watercolor 21¼" x 28¼"

J OHN PIKE BELIEVES that the most important thing is to paint on-the-spot wherever possible. When direct painting is impractical, Pike does black and white sketches on location, while thinking in color and aiding his memory with written color abbreviations.

In *Winter Evening*, Pike demonstrates his technique and illustrates some of the problems of painting a subject in early evening light. Although the watercolor was relatively easy to paint—with simple forms and only three major values, plus the very dark accents—it was a problem to come as close as possible to true value relationships. Great accuracy in these relationships is demanded by the very simplicity of the painting: white snow, white house against the brilliant sky— each in its proper place in the value scale between the lightest light (the sky) and the darkest darks (trees, shutters, and darks at the edge of the stream).

In painting the sky, Pike turned the paper upside down and started with a very pale wash of cadmium yellow medium, carefully avoiding the house and snow, as the yellow to the west has virtually no influence on their color. As he worked the yellow wash upward, he started to drop in a small amount of cold blue—Winsor or monastral. This was done very rapidly so that the paper would still be wet to produce soft edges when he touched in the fleeting clouds with a little Payne's gray.

The horizontal plane of the snow in the middle ground and foreground was affected only slightly by the yellow light of the distant horizon, since the main color influence is from directly above, except for the icy spots and the clear reflecting area of the stream. The vertical planes of the house and the distant hill gain their color and value almost entirely from the sky behind the viewer's back. Keeping in mind these influences, Pike painted the snow areas in blue-grays (ultramarine, Winsor blue, and Payne's gray), allowing a little cold green (viridian or similar) to hit on the flatter areas. The white house would naturally be darker in value and grayer in color than the luminous, reflecting snow. He painted in the house, leaving the white paper in the window for a later treatment. In the windows, he wanted to avoid the "look through" character and make the light come from within the house itself. The light from the sky is a direct light, but the light from the windows is indirect, reflecting from walls across the room and edges of curtains. They were dark in value and warm in color, so he used burnt sienna with a touch of cadmium yellow. The green of the shades was a cold green over the warm tone.

In the final stage, the artist painted in the trees, the darks in the right foreground, and the twigs and branches that pushed up through the snow. In doing the clear reflections, he advises painting the object first, then the reflection, in order to allow greater freedom in creating the forms.

Henry C. Pitz

Hidden Valley
Watercolor and ink 22¾" x 30½"
Collection, Norfolk Museum of Arts and Sciences

Using on-the-spot sketches made in pencil or crayon, Henry Pitz generally completes his paintings in his studio. *Hidden Valley*—the painting reproduced here—was painted in his studio from a small sketch he had made on location out west. It is essentially a wet wash with ink lines set into pools of watercolor, which he painted on a 300 lb imported paper.

Pitz does not favor an excessive number of colors, restricting his palette of tube watercolors to raw umber; yellow ochre; sometimes sepia or Van Dyke brown; Prussian blue; ultramarine blue; cadmium red; cadmium orange; cadmium yellow; and sometimes lemon yellow and Payne's gray. He paints primarily with red sables, which range in size from no. 3 up to at least no. 12. Occasionally, he uses a bristle brush, a housepainter's brush, or a Japanese brush for linear effects. He saves all his old brushes for dry-brush work, taking advantage of the interesting effects achieved by the worn, splayed bristles. In his studio, he places his sheet on a flat table top so that he can spread his washes easily. Pitz produces his paintings rapidly, perhaps in a couple of hours; occasionally he lets a wash dry overnight and completes it in a second session the following day.

Although Pitz never uses tricks that are flashy—overwhelming the painting in any way—he does use a few techniques for special effects. To achieve a crinkly texture, for example, he sometimes pours table salt on a wash fairly heavy with pigment. The salt repels colors in certain areas and clots these in other areas, producing an over-all mottled texture which is very effective for depicting a wall on an old building. Occasionally, he drops a little turpentine into a wash to achieve a light colored spot, a technique which can give a starry effect to a dark sky. To achieve another kind of textural effect, he may dip crinkled paper into casein, then press the paper template over a dried wash, which will create an appealing irregularity in the final texture.

142 Odgen M. Pleissner

Pont St. Benezet
Watercolor 18" x 28"
Collection, Alfred E. Bissell

Ogden PLEISSNER PAINTS most of his finished watercolors in his studio from small 7" x 10" color sketches, quite complete in form, which he makes on the spot. Sometimes—depending on the conditions under which he must work—he finds it more convenient to make preliminary sepia pen and wash drawings or pencil sketches with color notations. Under reasonable weather, Pleissner prefers to work before his subject in color. Though he often makes small watercolors as studies, occasionally he paints half sheets (15" x 21"), while standing and working on an easel.

For large watercolors, Pleissner uses a 300 lb English all-rag paper, rough surface. For working out-of-doors, he has paper made up in blocks of half sheets, in 200 lb stock, and the smaller 7" x 10" sheets, in blocks of 140 lb cold pressed stock. Since he cannot abide wrinkled paper, he always stretches the full sheets of 300 lb paper when working in his studio.

First, he submerges the sheet in a tub of cold water (hot or even warm water removes too much of the size) for fifteen minutes. Then the paper is placed on a drawing board and the excess water blotted, not rubbed from the surface, with a clean towel. After the edges of the sheet are carefully dried, Pleissner tapes down the paper on all four sides with heavy gummed paper strips, 2" wide. He exerts pressure on the tape by rubbing it vigorously with a soup spoon, otherwise the whole business would buckle. On top of this first set of strips, he affixes a second set in the same manner, to withstand the powerful contraction of the paper.

Generally, he stretches his paper a day before painting. Sometimes, he makes a light linear drawing on a dry stock before it is stretched, and in this case he begins working in color before it has completely dried. He can obtain special effects when the paper surface is damp.

Pleissner uses watercolor paint in tube form in the following colors: cadmium lemon, cadmium pale, cadmium medium, cadmium orange, cadmium scarlet, ivory black, Payne's gray, sepia, yellow ochre, raw sienna, burnt sienna, raw umber, burnt umber, light red, Winsor green, Winsor blue, permanent blue, cobalt, and cerulean blue; occasionally, he adds alizarin crimson, managanese blue, viridian, terre verte, new gamboge yellow, and permanent white. He uses a palette which is specially designed to keep colors moist when not in use. His mixing palette in the studio is the porcelain top of a small kitchen table.

Before he begins to paint a full sheet, Pleissner makes a preliminary line drawing on tracing paper to completely establish the design and perspective. This in turn is transferred to his watercolor paper. This transfer process keeps the watercolor paper free from erasures and extraneous lines which would occur if he attempted a direct drawing enlargement from his smaller studies, especially in the architectural subjects he often undertakes.

Nathaniel Pousette-Dart

Woodstock
Watercolor   14" x 20"

Watercolors painted by Nathaniel Pousette-Dart (1886–1965) look as if they had been done easily. This is not the case, however. His first attempts at watercolor were complete failures, probably because he tried to do them in the accepted loose-flowing way. It was not until he resorted to the additional use of pen and ink that he started to gain control over his medium. To him, the pen and ink acted as a stabilizer. With it, he was able more fully to realize the form, to coordinate the textures, and to complete the organization of his watercolors.

Pousette-Dart had no set procedure in working. Sometimes he made a very careful pencil drawing, over which he worked in pen and ink, adding color when the line work was completed. At other times, he drew his subject directly in pen and ink and then worked into it with watercolors. He sometimes finished a watercolor in one sitting, at other occasions he worked on it twenty or more times. If it proved unusually refractory, he soaked it in the bathtub and took out large sections—because freshness, he was convinced, comes not from ease and rapidity of workmanship, but from right relationships which are sometimes achieved only after extensive experimentation.

There is only one thing that he tried to do religiously, and that was to work in watercolor only when he felt inspired, for only at such times did every stroke of his pen, pencil, or brush become an essential part of the whole work.

Pousette-Dart admitted that the right kind of paper, colors, pens, or brushes might make the difference between the success and failure for an individual artist, but Pousette-Dart really felt that materials are of secondary importance. He found that his best work was done when he had thought about a subject for a long time before starting to paint it. Long and loving consideration ripens naturally into inspiration, and at such times the work seems to do itself, unhindered by intellectual interference. When he was ready to paint, the subject itself suggested the colors for his palette, the most suitable paper, and the right brushes. "The longer I work on watercolors," the artist once stated, "the more abstract they become. This is probably due to a subconscious desire to eliminate everything which is accidental and irrelevant. Nature is profuse and chaotic, whereas a work of art is a completely organized thing existing within its own well-defined limitations." This kind of logic was reflected in his work.

Adds use of pen & ink

Sets only areas to be painted!
Tends to be abstract.

146   Noel Quinn

Noel quinn does the majority of his paintings on the spot and in one sitting. He seldom makes preliminary sketches or rough layouts, because he wants to spend his feelings on the watercolor itself. He indicates the placement of the big shapes by noting key dots and lines and, within these, he suggests the way in which the forms relate to each other. He paints boldly and directly, attacking the subject matter with confidence and vigor.

The artist's approach is based largely on color. Quinn begins at once to brush in the large masses of color, dark against light, light against dark. These make interesting vibrations of color and value working together within the large shapes. The design element in his paintings is basically abstract. He brings the areas of the painting into focus only in the finishing stages, although he believes that the design must be exciting in itself from the start. On occasion, he enjoys working into areas of the painting with detail and texture. However, the basic form remains simple and an integral part of the whole.

Quinn uses top quality, 300 lb watercolor paper, a paper that will take rough handling and allows considerable wetness without buckling. He generally works on a full sheet, 22" x 30", but only wets the area about to be painted. This calculated process of saturation gives him considerable control of the white areas, a factor which is important to Quinn because he uses the whites of his paper as very definite passages of color value.

For a working palette, Quinn uses two stainless steel mess trays hinged together. The deep wells are excellent for mixing many colors and washes. On field trips, he carries water in a hot water bottle. Rather than bring a big umbrella for painting outdoors, he wears sunglasses with calobar lenses. Surprisingly, they do not affect his sense of color and are also helpful in simplifying values.

Quinn's principle color palette is simple: Prussian or phthalocyanine blue, alizarin crimson, burnt sienna, raw sienna, yellow ochre, burnt umber, viridian, monastral green, cadmium red light, cadmium yellow pale, Payne's gray, and neutral tint.

The artist uses a fair number of red sable brushes, including three or four of the no. 12 and two of the no. 30. Although expensive, these jumbo sables are long lasting and unbeatable for the initial color punch, as well as for the succeeding overlays of color wash which tie the picture together.

148   Marques E. Reitzel

Bᴇꜰᴏʀᴇ ꜱᴛᴀʀᴛɪɴɢ ᴀ ᴘᴀɪɴᴛɪɴɢ, Marques Reitzel (1896–1967) liked to consider the subject from various angles and frequently made as many as ten or twelve preliminary sketches. These varied in size from thumbnail compositions to full scale drawings the size of the projected watercolor. He used soft graphite pencil for line studies and carbon pencil for those executed principally in tone. With all his sketches close at hand for easy reference, he was able to start his painting with confidence.

Reitzel's palette consisted of lemon yellow, cadmium yellow pale, cadmium orange, cadmium red or vermilion, alizarin crimson, Hooker's green, cobalt blue, French ultramarine blue, Prussian blue, charcoal gray, yellow ochre, raw and burnt sienna, raw and burnt umber—and occasionally he added Payne's gray and viridian.

In setting this palette for use, he favored a white enamel tray, 16″ x 20″, placing the colors on its rim and using the large central portion for a mixing area. This allowed him to see clearly the density of his mixture, and helped to avoid errors in saturation before applying color to the paper. For his brushes, Reitzel used a no. 12 round sable and a 1″ flat sable for the major work. For painting details, he needed only two or three smaller ones of similar quality. He liked to stand while he painted outdoors, so he used a folding easel (adaptable for both oil and watercolor).

Since most of his watercolors were executed in the wet-in-wet technique, Reitzel found that an all-rag 300 lb paper did not buckle when he subjected it to a thorough wetting with a large natural sponge—a process that usually took about twenty minutes. Also, its heavy weight did not require stretching; and the paper held its saturation for about an hour and a half, drying remarkably even.

Just as soon as the wet surface received the color, Reitzel generally began his painting by putting down the lightest colors and gradually building up to the deepest ones with darkest values at the last. This timing requires a great deal of patience and skill. In the early stages, the larger areas of light tones fused and bled, providing airy effects of atmosphere. As the paper lost its heaviest saturation (by drying), more definition of form was managed, and it is at this point that he used a dry-brush technique—a full brush of color with practically no water added —to strike in textures and forms that required definite accent to bring the whole work into pictorial focus. Painting in the wet method calls for a bold attack without hesitation, and it is for this reason that the preliminary sketches are so vital to a progressive painting process.

Art Riley

Vincent Thomas Bridge
Watercolor 21" x 29"

For art riley, *Vincent Thomas Bridge*—a favorite subject which he has painted many times—has two major elements that seem directly opposed: on the one hand, its great surging strength; and on the other, the apparent delicacy of its tracery of cables and catwalks. It was this contrast that he tried to capture in his series of paintings of the bridge.

Working on a full sheet of heavy, imported French paper, Riley used pen and ink to establish the basic structure of the bridge and its complicated perspective, before he began to use any color wash. Although he works rapidly, the complexity of the subject often required five hours of concentrated effort for him to complete any of his watercolors of the bridge. Even so, his large watercolor sheet looked like a tiny sketch pad in comparison to the towering elements of the bridge.

Like most experienced professionals, Riley uses the best artists' materials available: permanent colors, the finest papers, and a generous supply of sable brushes. Because of the architectural demands of the bridge subject, he found that the chisel edged brush was the best to employ for all the straight edges and planes; and for the tracery of cables and other similar detail, a sign writer's striping brush. For certain areas which he wanted to reserve for subsequent painting, he used broad mending tape in a frisket fashion—washed *over* this with color, and then, when the surrounding area was dry, the tape was removed.

used a stripping brush for cables
and tape for straight-effect
formating

152   Morton Roberts

Morton Roberts

Portsmouth, New Hampshire
Watercolor 22" x 30"
Collection, Herbert L. Pratt

In THIS DECEPTIVELY SIMPLE WATERCOLOR, Morton Roberts (1927-1964) used a wide variety of techniques which demonstrate his versatility and skill.

A wet-in-wet technique was employed for the trees in the upper right hand corner, where the dark and light tones flow into one another, and the tree trunks have been painted into the wet green so that the edges of the trunks blend with the foliage. See how the rough paper breaks through here and there as the brush skims over the surface leaving flecks of white to indicate the light coming through the branches. The tree trunks themselves seem to be painted with a single broad stroke of a brush charged with two colors, one warm and one cool. Here and there a branch is picked out with a scraping tool—perhaps a knife or brush handle—which cuts through to the white of the paper. At certain places the wet-in-wet of the foliage gives way to dry-brush.

Dry-brush is used extensively for the very delicate strokes that pick out the architectural details of the white house and the fence. Here the white is simply the paper which shines through the strokes but is very delicately modified by pale washes of cool shadow tones. Notice how these shadows sometimes move from cool to warm, to create greater variety within the predominantly cool tones.

Dry-brush is also used extensively in the foreground where the rough texture in the pavement is indicated by short, rough strokes, laid over a preliminary color wash.

The artist's selective use of detail is also interesting. Some of the windows, for example, are carried into much greater detail than others; the same is true of the boards of the building and fence. In some cases, just a patch of color will do, while in others the details are defined with crisp lines and firm edges.

The dramatic composition lends excitement to what is inherently a static subject; its swift perspective sweeps the viewer back into the distance, past the houses and fence into the darkness of the trees.

Alex Ross

The Birth of Eve
Watercolor 20" x 27¾"
Collection, Mattatuck Museum

Over the years, Alex Ross has learned to become master of what he calls his "little helpers"; namely, brushes, pigments, sponges, razor blades, salt, water, turpentine, and soap. There is one material he will not use: rubber cement, or its various derivatives. Although he has used rubber cement in the past, he now looks upon it with distaste because the results are so glaringly obvious to him.

Alex Ross uses medium weight bond paper and a black pencil for preliminary sketches. When he is satisfied with the over-all design, he makes a rough pencil sketch of the entire picture to determine the pattern, the black and white values, and a focal point, if necessary. Following this, he makes one or two, and sometimes more, color sketches based on a tonal structure of the pencil sketch. This build-up is necessary if he is to begin his painting with confidence.

Next, he prepares the working surface by soaking heavy weight watercolor paper in water, taping it to a plywood board, and allowing it to dry. He begins to paint by roughing in dark areas with a watery casein mixture. Once the casein dries, it is more apt to hold the image under succeeding washes than if he had used a watercolor underpainting; dry casein is relatively insoluble in water, whereas dried watercolor may dissolve in the next wash applied.

For off-beat effects, turpentine mixed with water has become a particular favorite with Ross. Sometimes he adds soap to watercolor to facilitate control; the heavier consistency of the soap changes the brushing consistency of the paint. (The old masters sometimes did this with starch.) He also frequently uses a banker's pen loaded with black casein watered to an ink-like consistency and applied to wet ground, which produces a line that surprises the artist by giving him "controlled accidents" in a lively, unpredictable pen line. He tries to avoid sponging or wiping out areas of color that have become muddy or overworked, preferring to start over again, unless he thinks it might be possible to rework an area with good results.

According to george samerjan, the most valuable habit he has cultivated is the "sketchbook habit." Wherever he goes, he carries the little pocket sketchbook. In it he jots down basic information about any subject that impresses him. Later, when he makes a painting from the sketch, he is less likely to become involved in unnecessary details. After many years of painting wholly on location, Samerjan now prefers to work from notes and sketches, developing the picture in his studio. When painting, Samerjan tries to be so organized that he can put every bit of fire and enthusiasm into the painting without being dissipated by distractions.

Before he begins to paint in his studio, Samerjan puts out all necessary equipment. He pours tube colors fresh into a partition-type watercolor palette. Nearby, he keeps a gallon of fresh water, and a worn-out towel to keep his hands and brushes clean and dry. A large vase full of brushes is handy. Although many brushes of all sizes and shapes have accumulated over the years, he probably employs only two or three on any one painting. He uses a silk sponge for lifting and controlling color that might float "out of drawing." He also has handy a bottle of India ink, Speedball pen points, and a supply of watercolor paper.

First, Samerjan usually sponges his 300 lb paper, then removes excess water carefully with the sponge. The large masses of color are brushed in quickly and vigorously. He continues to draw into the masses with additional color as the painting develops, keeping the sponge ready for any adjustment that may be required. Color is removed only when he decides that there is no possible alternative. Watercolor suffers greatly in brilliance and luminosity when it is "disturbed," so he avoids scrubbing as much as possible.

After he has reached the point where the paper is completely covered and the basic concept of the painting has been indicated, he keeps the picture "working" all over; otherwise he loses some areas and overdevelops others. By laying in the entire paper at the very beginning, he is able to maintain uniformity.

After the lay-in, refinements are planned with extreme care. Several times he steps back six to eight feet to evaluate the work. From a distance, this evaluation reveals legibility, color quality, design, and over-all effect. Further manipulation is then undertaken with surgical care, avoiding the danger of overworking, or "noodling" and muddying the color. If he needs to lower the tone of a passage, he must do it while the wash will be accepted by the paper. This stage of painting he feels is the most critical.

Although he has set up the watercolor at this point, the painting is primarily a pattern of color without much definitive drawing. At this stage, he begins to draw with India ink—a fact he has anticipated throughout the whole stage of painting. This pen point provides both fine and broad lines, depending on the way it is used, and the artist feels that it contributes an exciting calligraphic quality.

Joseph L. C. Santoro

Pounding Surf
Watercolor 22" x 28"

When working outdoors, Joseph Santoro staples his paper onto a lightweight drawing board. Before beginning a pencil sketch, he spends time trying to reduce the scene to a simple denominator, searching for a single characteristic that projects the theme and mood. He looks for large areas which can be reduced to massive washes in a bold manner, but he does not isolate or mask out an area by painting around it. Instead, he prefers using a broad, free stroke with a very large brush, returning later to add detail over the original wash. If necessary, he sponges out the area in which detail is to be placed.

He paints on a wet or on a dry surface, depending largely on the subject and the effect he wishes to achieve. For example, if the painting includes a large sky area, he wets this passage thoroughly, allowing the colors to blend readily, avoiding sharp delineations which would tend to bring the sky areas (optically) into the foreground.

There are also times when he prefers to do certain parts of a painting in damp, broad washes as underpainting. A dampened surface permits glazing with additional colors without becoming muddy. Since color painted on a wet surface will generally dry to a much lighter value, he tries to have the values well established in his mind before soaking that section of the paper so that colors may be applied rapidly. Of course, the more water used, the less brilliant the color will be when it dries.

He finds an underpainting useful on occasion. For example, huge rocks, with their varying color combinations from darks to lights, call for the admixture of countless colors. All this usually requires the step-by-step build-up of tone. However, when he wants to capture a thrashing surf or wild eddies, there is time only for a broad sweeping brush well loaded with color. Later, after studying the painting, he washes out an area with a sponge and, if necessary, resorts to bristle brushes, steel wool pad, or even sandpaper.

Santoro uses a 400 lb, 22" x 30" cold pressed (medium) watercolor paper. He feels he can depend on this heavy weight surface to take the toughest treatment technically and still provide a highly workable surface.

Santoro's watercolor box is jumbo size, opening to 20" x 22" to allow ample mixing area and some large paint wells. He prefers to use large amounts of color and therefore purchases professional grade, studio size tubes. His palette includes cadmium yellow light, raw sienna, cadmium orange, vermilion, cadmium red deep, alizarin crimson, burnt umber, raw umber, cerulean blue, cobalt blue, French ultramarine blue, Winsor green, Winsor blue, Payne's gray. On occasion, he uses opaque casein, providing it can be made part of the whole color pattern and not just added for a highlight.

Betty Lou Schlemm

Lanesville
Watercolor 21½" x 28½"

BEFORE HER FIRST STROKE IS MADE, Betty Lou Schlemm studies the scene and attempts to capture its essence. Is it hot, cold, or merely cool? Is it quiet and dignified, or raucous and flamboyant? She uses any pencil handy, soft or hard. The artist disagrees strongly with the approach of creating "happy accidents," and insists on disciplined painting and keeping design uppermost in her mind.

She has no preference between wet and dry methods, although she probably tends to paint more dry than wet. The artist likes to work with 300 lb paper whenever she can afford it. Her favorite brush is the rotary—a single brush with a ½" flat at one end and a no. 8 round at the other. She paints outdoors quite often, and finds the rotary extremely helpful in her work, because it allows her to change from the flat to the round quickly with a minimum of fuss before the sun dries the paper.

Her palette consists of Winsor red, cadmium orange, lemon yellow, ultramarine blue, cerulean blue, alizarin crimson, and most of the earth colors. In the beginning, she often uses ivory black, very diluted, to mark off large areas of dark values and usually ends a painting by emphasizing these accents. (What she is really trying to achieve in a painting is to capture the wind and to imprison it on paper.) When painting, she lays wash over wash of color on the same area in order to evaluate one color against another.

This procedure varies in time: sometimes it consumes only an hour, at other times a full day, or more. Very often she takes a piece of work back to the studio for final touches to pull everything together. Executing a painting drains her both physically and emotionally: something more than paint leaves the brush during a session; it is a part of the artist.

Carl Setterberg

Fishing Boats, Takamatsu
Watercolor 18" x 25½"

ACCORDING TO CARL SETTERBERG, planning a painting—especially the composition —before the actual brush strokes are applied is of utmost importance. The painting must be well organized and well thought out so that the shapes and patterns will not break up. Setterberg generally makes several thumbnail sketches before he establishes the final plan. He also finds that a small preliminary sketch, containing values and color notes, is sound procedure. Setterberg frequently makes quick sketches in the field, which he develops later in the studio, a practice he feels is good for developing a visual memory. He has a collection of these sketches in the studio and frequently resorts to them for inspiration.

To collect material for his paintings, the artist frequently carries an old Leica which he can easily slip into his pocket. He exploits its wide-angle lens to take a panoramic picture from which he can select whatever he may wish to paint— eliminating, exaggerating, changing perspective and composition, adding figure suggestions. He guards against following the photo too literally, always endeavoring to interpret its form but not to copy it.

Setterberg uses only a moderate number of colors on his palette. In fact, one weekend in the Adirondacks he discovered that he had forgotten his tube colors and was obliged to get along with the few in his watercolor box: yellow ochre, brown madder, Hooker's green dark, and Payne's gray. He found that this limited palette proved quite adequate. He believes that the use of too many colors can often make the total color impression ineffective.

He recommends only the finest quality watercolors, paper, and brushes. The fear of ruining a clean expanse of good paper is a great hazard for the beginner to surmount, Setterberg feels, so he suggests the economy of using the reverse side of the sheet if the first attempt is unsatisfactory. This artist uses a cellulose sponge for soaking up superfluous moisture in the brush and Kleenex for blotting or lifting a color or for removing a color before it dries.

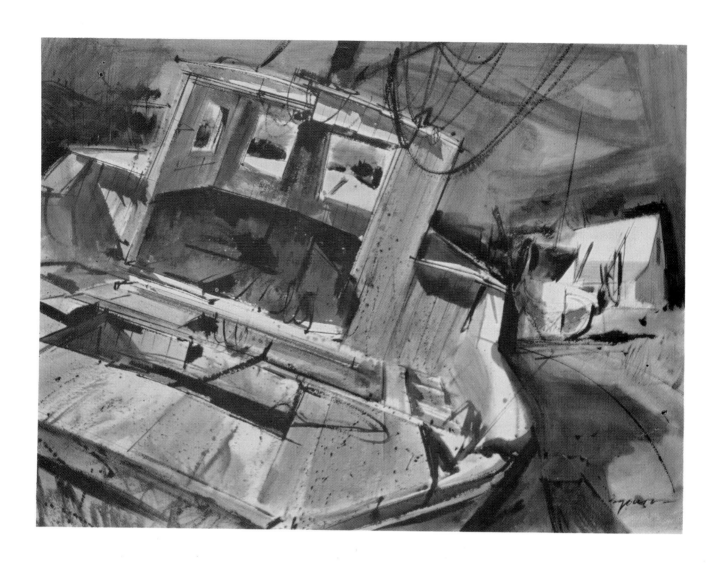

164 Thomas A. Sgouros

During the winter months, Thomas Sgouros usually works on large, deliberate paintings in oil. This turns out to be a slow and sometimes tedious task, since it loads his studio with uncompleted canvases. When he paints in watercolor (on location), his direct painting method makes it possible for him to complete a picture in one sitting. Decisions are reached quickly with no time for second guessing.

Although he is not governed too much by the subject before him, Sgouros finds that he does need it for his inspiration. Beyond that, he usually sacrifices its circumstantial arrangement, even its light and color, for those properties which are currently important to him—an interesting flat pattern and design on the surface of his paper. He cares very little for recording the precise scene; rather, he prefers to arrange arbitrarily what he sees before him into a unified design, even though the process often induces a certain amount of frustration, despair, and anguish.

Sgouros' method in painting a watercolor out-of-doors seldom varies. When he has found a stimulating subject, he begins immediately to plot his design by drawing in black ink on a sheet of 300 lb rough surfaced paper. At this stage, his tool is a long-handled oil brush. With this initial design completed, he turns to a combination of bristle brushes, sable brushes, and watercolor to produce the color washes—augmenting them, from time to time, with a sponge onto which he has poured colored dyes and inks. This rather unorthodox procedure, plus the fact that he works directly without preliminary sketches, generally results in a good deal of wasted paper, but when it is successful, the painting has a freshness and vitality he is unable to achieve any other way. However, when returning to the studio, if he finds that a particular watercolor needs adjustment—beyond the ideal he tries to achieve on the spot—he often works over the painted surface in pastel, to subdue or to highlight particular passages.

The watercolor reproduced on the facing paper was painted at Wellfleet, on Cape Cod. At the start of an intensive summer of painting, he decided to work with a severely limited palette in order to devote himself primarily to the problems of design and pattern. While he believes that self-imposed conditions rarely result in good paintings, he found that this discipline was valuable for *his* progress.

Irving shapiro prefers to work as directly as he can, arriving at the final result in one color wash wherever possible. This approach requires considerable forethought and visualization to know what can be done before the brush touches paper. Accents and suggestions of definition are usually added afterward, but not before the large masses are fairly complete in their statement.

His initial pencil drawing provides only a certain degree of guidance; the major portion of the drawing remains to be done with the brush. In this way, Shapiro finds a greater spontaneity in the final painting. Too literal and complete a pencil drawing restricts him from handling his materials with the zest and freedom he finds necessary for an animated result. He avoids becoming obsessed with useless detail, retaining a bold and dashing attitude in his approach.

Whenever possible, Shapiro gets outdoors to paint on the spot. At such times, he develops very brief color notes with, perhaps, a bit of pencil delineation added. A black and white photo taken of the subject, in combination with the color notes, will serve him adequately when he develops the painting in the studio—which is as soon after the original observation as possible. He frowns upon photos if the artist stops thinking and simply starts copying them.

Bus Stop was inspired by a passing glance at a mass of motorized metal that seemed animated with character to the artist. A photo of the bus, subsequent pencil roughs for composition and pattern, and plenty of enthusiasm produced the results we see reproduced here.

The challenges he faced in painting _Bus Stop_ included retaining the battered charm of the bus and complementing it with the interest of figure statements and suggestions. He felt that the introduction of the seated couple and the flower clusters provided a stronger foreground, thereby increasing the accentuation of the middle ground. The foil of massive dark in the background not only added strength, but again served as a contrasting element for the central interest.

Keeping all this in mind, Shapiro also felt the desire for an over-all feeling of warmth. In order to increase this quality, he washed over the entire paper surface with a very light, warm yellow prior to the painting of the solid forms. The influences and reflections thereby created a glow which pleased him.

The papers Shapiro uses are imported—all 300 or 400 lb rough stock. Such weights do away with the need for stretching. His brushes are nos. 8 and 12 round sable and two flat camel's hair, 1″ and 2″ wide. His palette consists of alizarin crimson golden, light vermilion, cadmium orange, cadmium yellow light, mauve, cobalt violet, phthalocyanine blue, ultramarine, cerulean, lemon yellow, sap green, phthalocyanine green, yellow ochre, burnt sienna, burnt umber, sepia, and Payne's gray.

Laurence Sisson

Boothbay Cove # 3
Watercolor 17" x 25½"
Collection, Mr. and Mrs. Robert Toppan

Laurence sisson came upon watercolor quite gradually. His work in oils seemed to lack the two dimensional strength he was discovering in nature, so he began using some washes on cold pressed paper one summer to record big patterns of light and dark. As he proceeded with these drawings, he found that he had much more control with the softer watercolor brushes than with his stiffer bristle ones. On top of these free washes he drew a kind of detailed calligraphy with ink and a reed pen. He found something compelling about the freedom of the wash and the nervous, impulsive, tracery of the ink dancing on the surface.

Sisson works almost exclusively on stretched paper. Using a heavy drawing board, he tapes down thoroughly wet, full sheets of 140 lb cold pressed paper which he allows to dry completely before painting. The heavy board gives him a feeling of resistance which he likes. A rougher paper dictates a more direct kind of technique and, though he enjoys working on it occasionally, the nubble or grain interferes with his more two dimensional approach.

Sisson's equipment is purposely limited—the fewer tools the better. Three brushes served him for many years until he added a fourth that has given him a great deal of pleasure: a Japanese horsehair, 2" flat with a chisel edge. He uses a small, round, white plastic palette, and he places six or seven fresh colors on it each day. A Mason jar for water, an art gum, and a sponge complete his tools.

Sisson usually begins a watercolor with a large wash. He prefers not to draw with a pencil first on the white surface unless he has a definite, preconceived plan that requires some lines to keep him from forgetting important areas. But if there are white spaces to be left, he often indicates them in pencil. He eagerly awaits the direction in which this first color, puddle, brush stroke, or implied form will take. The major areas of the painting are covered in a few minutes with overlays, then forms are added; a definite image usually shapes up in about twenty minutes. This is not a race he is trying to win, but one that normally takes place in his particular technique. From then on, he may spend some hours studying the passages already painted. Forms that were once intended for a mass of trees may now become new forms as the painting emerges, until a cohesive design is finally accomplished.

One of the most beautiful
plg. galleries
Color excellent +
Composition "

170   Flora Smith

Flora smith generally makes several preparatory sketches of her subject before beginning the final painting, so that she is sufficiently familiar with the drawing and composition to work spontaneously.

Blue Angel, the painting reproduced on the facing page, was painted with waterproof inks rather than with watercolor paint, although much of her other work is done with watercolors in the traditional manner. She uses the ink technique when, as in this case, she wants to get the peculiar effect that results from combining waterproof ink with water. Waterproof ink has its definite advantages. A line or wash can be applied to paper and allowed to dry. Other washes can then be successfully superimposed with no disturbance to the underpainting.

Usually, Flora Smith stretches the paper on a drawing board, soaking the paper when using a heavy sheet, and securing the edges with gummed tape. She uses a great variety of papers as each gives a different result.

In the process of making the drawing, the artist brushes on clear water first in the areas where she wants to produce soft edged effects, or where she wants to force the color to spread—such as in the wings and the crown. The degree of wetness of the paper is very important; if too wet, the ink will run too far, and it will be necessary to blot it off, wait for it to dry, and start over again in the same place. If not wet enough, the result will be nothing but a soggy spot. She tries to brush on the clear water just the way she expects the ink to run, allowing a little for spreading.

Flora Smith begins her color work with reed pens sharpened to blunt or fine points as desired. She also uses pen and brush alternately. The pen may appear to be a pretty rigid tool for free watercolor rendering, but after experimenting with it, by turning it at various angles, using its sides as well as its points, it will be found to be a very flexible tool capable of many effects. Pen and brush lines are sharp where the paper is not wet and blur where the paper is moist.

The artist usually mixes her inks in clean bottles, diluting them with boiled water. If the pen or brush were dipped in full strength ink, the result would be too brilliant. When the ink is diluted, however, the brush or pen can be fully loaded with the desired color.

When painting, Flora Smith has a whole row of bottles of diluted color with a sample of each color on a white palette table in front of them so that she can identify the colors quickly. She dips the brush or pen deep into the bottle to be sure it is full of color, then wets the sections where she wants the color to run, allowing plenty of room for spreading, according to pattern. This method produces accidents that, if exploited intelligently, add to the fun in execution as well as to the charm of the technical result.

An interesting variation in texture can be achieved by the use of ordinary table salt. A little salt, sprinkled quickly on the surface before the ink has time to settle, produces many very strange and fascinating effects.

172   Jacob Getlar Smith

Jacob getlar smith (1898–1958) maintained that economy of materials should be the rule with watercolorists. Too many types of paper, brushes, paints, and too much unnecessary tackle—he maintained—confound the painter as well as the fisherman. The art of watercolor is simplicity itself. And Smith worked according to that principle.

He always painted on the finest watercolor paper—a 100% linen rag hand-made product—in at least 140 lb weight. He preferred a large palette, with plenty of room for mixing, on which he arranged his colors in a consistent, logical order from light to dark, with warm and cold colors on either side. He found that a half dozen brushes of various sizes and shapes were more than enough and depended on just one or two for the majority of his work. His collection contained five sable brushes and one hog's hair.

In painting, Smith concentrated on the original theme throughout. From the first pencil mark to the final brush stroke, he never let the original composition leave his mind. With each application of brush to paper, he asked himself, "Am I sticking to my original plan? Am I getting the mood of that first impact between the subject and myself, or am I wandering off the track?"

Finally, as the painting reached the point where it called for emphasis and greater clarification, he brought up heavy artillery in the form of accents and telling detail—particularly in the foreground. (He remarked that many students neglect their foregrounds and put all the emphasis in the middle distance.) Important as these final accents are, Smith preferred to go easy with them. He used them sparingly, in order to avoid littering the picture with unimportant hocus-pocus, as he called it. He stated once, "Your eyes should be able to glide from one form into another, dancing in and out of the entire design. No eye-traps should be present except those deliberately placed to call attention to the central idea." He followed this principle in his work.

He consciously avoided painting a picture that was too literal, because he felt that some things should be left to the imagination of the audience. "The tantalizing appeal of many an unfinished sketch is due to the fact that the mind can conjure up a picture more beautiful than most artists can paint."

174　Don Stone

WHEN DON STONE PAINTS a watercolor, the first thing he considers is the mood of the painting: whether it is gay or serious, for example, will determine whether the colors are exciting or soft, the lines active or slow moving. Next he considers the conception of the painting: would it be better as a panoramic or as a close-up? How much should be included and how much left out?

His next consideration is the drawing. Stone's watercolors evolve out of a series of black and white and occasionally small color sketches, which show the large abstract shapes and color masses of the design. After deciding which sketch will make the best composition, Stone makes a careful, detailed drawing in pencil on the watercolor paper, visualizing how he is going to apply the washes, and how the completed painting will look.

At this point, he considers the values: whether the picture will be built from light to dark, or from dark to light, a decision which will often be dictated by the subject matter. For example, a panoramic painting with a large sky, rolling hills, and sweeping field may necessitate a light to dark treatment. In using this approach, Stone covers the entire area with the correct values in a wet-in-wet technique. After the large areas are covered in this manner, he works with less water and more paint to indicate the textures and refinements.

A fragmentary object, such as a bait barrel or lobster pot, might call for a dark to light approach. Working from the center of interest out—overstating the darks and leaving the white of the paper—Stone glazes over the entire area to unify and pull it together. (In watercolor, a glaze is a transparent wash laid in over an underpainting or preliminary wash, applied in such a way as not to destroy the primary layer. Glazing is a difficult task and can produce muddiness, but when done properly it can unify the painting effectively.) In painting from dark to light, Stone uses the color in a dry brush manner, relying on drawing rather than on washes, but maintaining the spontaneity of the medium at the same time.

For his colors, Stone purchases large studio tubes of the highest quality: new gamboge yellow, yellow ochre, cadmium orange, cadmium red deep, brown madder, burnt sienna, raw umber, Winsor blue, ultramarine blue, and Payne's gray. Not a very large palette, but very effective.

He uses good brushes, but not necessarily the most expensive. They consist of nos. 3, 5, 8, 12, and 18 in round sable; and a 1" and 1¼" in the flat sign writer type, plus a large flat 2" wash brush.

He paints on 300 lb cold pressed, imported stock. He works on it in an almost upright position; this prevents the sun from striking the surface, which would change the values and dry out the washes too rapidly. The upright position of the paper also enables him to control the medium with greater ease, since the water can run in only one direction—down the sheet—and such runs are quickly blotted with tissue, which the artist prefers to a razor or sponge.

176 William Strosahl

Puerto Cabello
Watercolor 17" x 29"
Collection, Rosemary Strosahl

W<small>ILLIAM</small> <small>STROSAHL</small> <small>DOES</small> most of his painting only at night, after his children are in bed and after the day's work of art direction is behind him. To a great degree, this dictates his personal working pattern. To start a painting, he usually makes five or six layout sketches from projected color slides. These have been taken over the years, with watercolors in mind. Included in his film file are hundreds of details of rocks, fences, old houses, clouds. The slides are projected on a sheet of seamless paper 12' wide. Seated at his easel across the room, he gets a feeling of being back at that scene, of being a part of that mood again.

After deciding on his composition, Strosahl makes drawings of the main elements on a layout pad. These are used for small, light-and-shade color sketches, 4" x 5". He then turns off the projector and never refers to the slide again. Strosahl works directly on his large paper, which is a good grade of medium or rough 300 lb stock, drawing as quickly as he can with an India ink fountain pen. He may drag the back of the nib at a right angle to give a heavy, ragged line, or he may use the pen in the regular manner for a variety of thin lines. The pen, which is a type used to set down original music scores, is best for this because it is extremely flexible.

Having established the light, medium, and dark areas in his color sketch, he tackles whichever part of the painting is the largest or most difficult for him. If it doesn't come off as well as he hopes, he starts over.

Strosahl usually lays down his color directly, with little or no overpainting, sometimes obliterating the pen line, sometimes missing it here and there to get sparkle and liveliness. Opaque white is something he uses only when he paints in casein; he believes the two techniques should be kept apart. However, on a transparent watercolor, he will scratch, bite, or gouge to get a desired effect.

Working from slides, in the method just described, two things are important. First, Strosahl has never been trapped into copying the photograph, because he believes it is vital to use his own interpretation of the scene. Second, when he thinks he has finished his painting, he makes the compositional and subject sketches for his *next* painting immediately, so that he will avoid the intimidating feeling of staring at a blank sheet of paper at the next session.

Strosahl uses standard brushes: nos. 12 and 8 sable, and ½" and 1" riggers. These, with a few no. 5 Japanese brushes (for flicking in calligraphic accents), are his usual tools. On occasion, he has used a shaving brush (for short grass areas), or a 2" housepainter's sash brush (for large sky areas). The only other tool is a decrepit, almost square-nosed knife.

His palette contains alizarin crimson, phthalocyanine blue, cobalt blue, Payne's gray, yellow ochre, Hooker's green, cadmium yellow, burnt sienna, burnt umber, Van Dyke brown, and sap green. Sometimes, indigo blue or neutral gray is added to the palette, but only when the picture's mood seems to call for it.

Ernest T. Thompson

Strolling in the Park
Watercolor 14½" x 20½"
Collection, Roy M. Mason

Eʀɴᴇsᴛ ᴛʜᴏᴍᴘsᴏɴ ᴅᴏᴇs most of his watercolors from sketches made on-the-spot and developed later in his studio. His final black and white study is made with a carbon pencil and a white chalk pencil on a blue-gray paper about 6" long, drawn to the exact scale of his painting. He then stretches his paper—140 lb stock—on a plywood board. In dampening the paper, Thompson uses a large 7" white paint roller to apply the water on both sides of the sheet. Next he lays a frame with a glass over the saturated paper, allowing the sheet to absorb the water and expand for about ten minutes. He then binds the paper down with heavy gummed tape and staples the tape at four-inch intervals for safety's sake. This prolonged wetting of the sheet effectively stretches the paper. He sets the stretched paper on his portrait easel.

Next, Thompson places his sketch in a Balopticon projector, darkens the studio, and projects the basic shapes of the drawing onto the final watercolor sheet. While the image is projected, he draws over the shapes, recapturing the freedom of the original sketch in a few moments. He then refines the drawing before he proceeds with the painting.

Thompson prefers a horizontal painting surface to a vertical one, tilting the board only for gradation of tone. His painting procedure follows the normal pattern of working from the lightest to the darkest tone in the painting. The sky is generally the dominant tone of any landscape, so he prefers to paint it first because it is easier to relate the landscape to the sky than the reverse. The graded sky is divided into three basic color areas, from horizon to zenith, the colors being mixed in quantity in a three-compartment candy dish he keeps nearby. He prefers to work his skies upside down, by reversing the board and working downward from the horizon with the three washes applied in succession with overlapping tones, using a large 2½" flat white bristle enamel brush. By working directly and rapidly, he is able to avoid a labored surface. Thompson uses only top-quality paper, colors, and brushes, although he does suggest that ox hair brushes may be substituted for red sable in the larger sizes.

The artist uses a medium-sized sheet of white counter-top glass as a palette, periodically cleaning it with facial tissues during the painting process. His tube colors are placed in two porcelain slants, which in turn are placed on cellulose sponges that have been cemented to the bottom of a covered plastic refrigerator "meat saver" box. The sponges are dampened periodically with water to which carbolic acid is added (about ten drops to a pint). This prevents the formation of mold on the paint when the cover of the box is replaced and the colors are unused for a prolonged period. (His own paints remain moist for months at a time.) He often uses blotters to pick up and manipulate color, and a large hair dryer to accelerate the drying of washes.

180　William Thon

To WILLIAM THON, one of the most important things in watercolor is the white paper itself. When he starts out, he always plans to leave much of the paper untouched by color. He wets the paper completely first, using more than the usual amount of water, which he pours from a jug onto the paper. He likes to mix most of his colors on the wet paper, particularly at the start.

Although he does not make any drawing or outline in pencil or charcoal, Thon has his subject clearly in mind before he begins. He starts off with a color wash that will establish a sky or other main area of the composition. With a large brush (2" perhaps), rich with strong color, he begins at the top of the paper and works more or less down. For the smaller objects, he uses thinner brushes and usually a drier consistency of paint. Besides using brushes, he sometimes uses his finger. He also keeps razor blades, sponges, and tissues handy for mopping up or wiping off a color; for instance, after washing in the background, he may need to restore areas of the white paper so that he can work in other colors and masses of the main objects he wants to include in the picture.

By using a great deal of water, Thon gives himself as long a time as possible, before the color starts to dry, in which to decide exactly how he wants various areas to perform. With the paper tacked to a large drawing board, he is able to lift up the painting and tilt it this way or that to make the wash flow in the direction he wants. Thon keeps ahead of the drying of the paper, at least while the main part of the painting is being done. When the paper is drier (or completely dry), he may add crisp, sharp lines to outline objects more clearly, accent others perhaps with stronger color, and make other finishing touches which he feels will strengthen the painting. Usually, he works with quick, spontaneous strokes.

The contrast of wet color washes with fuzzy outlines and the more clearly defined lines made with a dry brush or with a quill pen and India ink can be most effective. Sometimes texture can be improved by the addition of color or, in a dark area, by a touch or two of white, or by the removal of some of the paint. Thon very seldom uses white paint, except to make another color lighter and more opaque; he prefers to employ the white of the paper for all necessary highlights. Color can be removed from a dry surface by scraping the paper gently with a razor blade. At other times, he wets an area for reworking. A good way to rewet a watercolor without disturbing the work is to use a Flit gun, or some other type of insect spray gun. He also often uses a sponge, which will absorb some of the remoistened paint, and gives him greater control in small areas.

Thon can work on a watercolor every day for a week without making it appeared labored. And he can return to it months or years later to make changes he desires, by sponging out parts of the picture for repainting. He does all his finished work indoors, away from the sun and wind.

Jack Vallee

Wet Sand
Watercolor 20½" x 28"
Collection, Mr. and Mrs. Joseph Cox

When he paints in his studio—depicting a subject based on an idea rather than on concrete form—Jack Vallee sketches variations of his idea, then selects the sketch that best projects the image. With a lead pencil, he draws light structure lines on 300 lb, 22" x 30" cold pressed paper, working on a drawing board. After sketching out his composition, he places the sheet of paper across the room to remove it from the surroundings in which he has been working. This helps him analyze the application of the washes, especially their values and intensities (which are subject to change as the painting progresses), and to clarify the feeling he wants to convey.

During these indoor sessions, Vallee works with large watercolor palettes to facilitate big, clean washes. First, he generally moistens the entire paper with a brush or sponge, though sometimes it is only necessary to dampen one area at a time, depending on the control he desires.

During the painting session (usually five to eight hours), Vallee tries to keep his approach objective by turning the painting upside down and looking at it in the mirror to see it inverted. After the basic statement has been completed, he stops for the time being, although he may return later for a brief session.

Vallee's materials include all sizes and shapes of sable brushes; two sign painter's brushes; a sponge for dampening the paper, for daubing in light areas, or for brushing in paint to achieve particular effects; a rag or damp chamois for rubbing out colors; a pocket knife for removing wet color (by a squeezing motion) to produce light areas and shapes; a single-edged razor blade to scrape parts of the watercolor down to the white base after the painting has dried. His palette consists of tubes of cadmium yellow, yellow ochre, vermilion, raw sienna, burnt sienna, burnt umber, Hooker's green dark, ultramarine, phthalocyanine blue, and charcoal gray.

For location painting, Vallee recommends 4B and 6B lead pencils, a medium-sized sketch pad, a large 140 lb watercolor block, a small portable palette, a hand mirror, a camp stool, an army canteen with a detachable cup, and the type of brushes and paints mentioned above. This gear is highly portable and will enable the painter to move from subject to subject with little difficulty.

His method for on-the-spot painting is somewhat different from his method in the studio. Vallee makes quick, fluid preliminary sketches with a pencil, and then sketches construction lines on the watercolor block. After a period of contemplation, as in studio painting, Vallee begins painting the washes in as direct and simple a manner as possible, trying to arrive at the key to his particular feeling for the subject. All this takes two to three hours. Then he returns to the studio to study the painting, and possibly to make adjustments.

Ferdinand Wagner

Smith Falls
Watercolor 14½" x 21"
Collection, Norman Kent

Ferdinand wagner always carries a sketchbook, pocket size or larger, to jot down notes when the creative spirit moves him. Whenever he drives, he takes all his equipment. He likes to paint watercolors on the spot, where he has subject matter at hand, often recomposing or inventing landscape composition by taking a tree from one place, a rock from another, a barn or house from still another. He usually knows exactly what he plans to do before setting up his easel, since often he studies the possibilities for a long time before he begins to paint.

Wagner's easel is a strong tripod with retractable legs which can be adjusted to any terrain. A lightweight table of his own design and make is attached. His favorite paper is a 300 lb imported rag stock, which he attaches to a lightweight board with gummed tape. He likes to paint in a standing position for greater freedom of movement. After drawing the subject with the easel tilted at a right angle to the line of vision, he always moves it back to the horizontal position for painting; this is important in watercolor painting because it facilitates control of the flow of color. For this reason, the screw which holds the board at the desired angle is never kept too tight.

A muffin tin with twelve small wells holds Wagner's colors. He also uses white, baked enamel mixing trays, two nesting aluminum cups (from a gallon thermos jug), and a discarded plastic detergent container for his water. All his equipment is packed in an expanding portfolio. He likes large brushes, especially the jumbo size wash type which will hold plenty of color and still retain a good point. Wagner often makes entire paintings with just one brush. In addition, he feels that wonderful effects can be achieved by applying color with a fine sponge. He finds an atomizer handy for moistening areas that have dried too much, and a knife for scraping. He also uses a chisel-shaped, plastic gadget to squeegee through wet painted areas; with this edge, he can indicate tree trunks and branches out of a toned, wet background.

Smith Falls, the painting reproduced here, was painted in the manner Wagner likes best: no tricks, just a straightforward approach to a challenging subject, with a limited palette of transparent colors. This palette contained simply Hooker's green, Winsor blue, alizarin crimson, raw sienna, and burnt sienna, but no black, white, or opaques. In fact, he never uses any but pure transparent colors. He knew what he was going to do with this picture because he had previously painted the same subject a number of times. This time he planned to simplify, to achieve a complete painting without fussy details. As a result, the entire painting was done with his jumbo wash brush on dry paper, with only an occasional use of a small sponge to dampen areas he wanted to blend.

For john walsh, a painting must be executed quite rapidly, or it will end up lacking the verve and spontaneity he always tries to achieve. Ideally, he prefers to do several black and white or pastel sketches before beginning to paint. He also likes to gaze at a subject, especially from a hotel window. After a few days of breakfasting before an open window, the main elements of the scene below tend to arrange themselves in the subconscious mind without effort, and the final painting is practically prefabricated before he starts.

The picture reproduced here in color is, however, an exception to this procedure. It was done without any preliminaries and started within fifteen minutes of checking into a hotel in Portugal. The late afternoon sun was lighting up the curving waterfront and roof tops, seen through a small casement window. The mood was right, the comparison ready-made, and the first impression so strong that something had to be done about it right away.

For such work on the spot, Walsh generally uses a half sheet, lightly taped to a board. In the studio, with adjustable table and bigger palette available, larger sizes can be painted almost as quickly. Inside or outside, all his technique and equipment are aimed at getting the paint onto the surface with the least delay. For this reason, he shies away from heavy weight papers which do not take the color easily without a good deal of scrubbing, and instead he uses a relatively light and absorbent rag paper. Though he has to put up with the inevitable buckling and the impossibility of making large erasures, this seems to suit him much better.

Walsh uses two or three flat sables and some small round brushes for finer strokes. His usual palette contains ultramarine, cobalt and Prussian blues, yellow ochre, cadmium pale, light and medium yellows, cadmium orange and red, light red, alizarin crimson, Hooker's no. 1, raw umber, Payne's gray, and ivory black.

For speed of working, Walsh sometimes dampens the whole surface and works wet from beginning to end. More often, he dampens only certain large areas such as sky or water, setting the general color scheme with such elements, then working the other colors in relation to them, from light to dark. Towards the end, he adds any intense color spots or accents which may be required and applies dark or black lines with brush or felt pens. He aims for transparent color throughout, but does not hesitate to employ body color for light accents or texture. Later, in the studio, he adds a few final touches and, if necessary, a little light overpainting here and there to modify or unify the design and color scheme. This phase often takes longer than the main part of the work. Like most watercolorists, he finds that he has to hold himself back to avoid overfinishing.

John C. Wenrich

In the Yards
Watercolor 17⅜" x 24⅜"

In HIS MANY YEARS of making architectural renderings, John Wenrich has, of necessity, developed a detailed type of painting. It has always been a challenge to him to show a good deal of detail, without the viewer being conscious of this feature. He has to plan every square inch of his compositions.

To acquire material, Wenrich has made many trips, doing drawings and color sketches on-the-spot, though he usually develops his finished compositions in his studio. He first plans his composition by making thumbnail sketches, then carefully draws his subject full size. Darkest colors are laid in first. Then he gets the white paper covered with thin washes as quickly as possible, and gets down to the business of final color values.

Wenrich admits that his palette is somewhat larger than necessary. For reds, he uses alizarin crimson, vermilion, and Venetian red; for yellows, cadmium regular and light; for greens, Winsor, Hooker's no. 2, and oxide of chromium; for blues, Prussian, ultramarine, cobalt, and cerulean; for earth colors, burnt and raw sienna and raw umber; for neutralizers, Payne's gray and charcoal gray; and for occasional admixture, ivory black and Chinese white.

Wenrich's brushes are red sable, both the pointed and square-end type, varying in size from small to very large. For paper, he uses imported boards, 300 lb all-rag stock of medium rough surface, and a variety of lightweight papers, which he carefully mounts on a secondary support, prior to painting. While his architectural renderings vary in size, depending on the demands of his clients, his easel pictures are usually in three sizes: 12" x 17", 15" x 22", and 18" x 24".

Though most of Wenrich's watercolors are executed in the transparent medium, he does not hesitate to introduce passages of gouache—a technique he uses primarily in his architectural renderings. The combination of tones is never circumstantial or employed for corrective purposes, but is calculated. More often than not, he uses the transparent wash for shadow planes and the more opaque gouache for illuminated surfaces and for creating weight and dimension.

FREDERIC WHITAKER.

190   Frederic Whitaker

Uphill Street
Watercolor 22″ x 30″

SOME ARTISTS PAINT IMPORTANT WORKS with nothing more to follow than a mental plan, developing details as they proceed, but Frederic Whitaker likes to work out every factor in advance. Instead of flooding paint over a full sheet of watercolor paper—corrections on which Whitaker feels are harder to correct than oil —he first makes a 5″ or 6″ full color sketch, using *gouache*, since it lends itself to making repeated changes rapidly, one passage on top of another. He continues adjusting the sketch in form, color, and value until the layout satisfies him completely. He says that, using this method, he can see his faults at a glance, but the remedy may escape him for some time.

The final step in this little pilot painting is to enclose its forms within certain desirable boundaries. This he feels is most important, since it is easier to move the borders to fit the picture material than it would be to shift the whole picture across the paper. Then too, in using this carefully worked out sketch as a basis for full sheet watercolor (a maximum of 22″ x 30″), Whitaker makes its dimensions fit the proportions of one of seven stock frame sizes. He and his artist wife Eileen have adopted these stock sizes of mat and frame combinations in order to minimize the difficulty of shifting their watercolor paintings from one frame to another. With all of his problems worked out in these small color sketches, Whitaker is able to paint the final watercolor confidently and without fumbling, assured of a good design, but creating an effect that gives the illusion of having been produced spontaneously.

In discussing his respect for, and dependence on, solid design, Fred Whitaker believes that the young painter learns the technique of applying paint early, but spends the rest of his life wrestling with conceptual and compositional problems. Design in a painting, he says, is the contrived arrangement of masses, colors, values, directions and key, which—when added to the chosen theme—are made to go together to make the composed picture. No photographic copy of a subject can do that, for pictures, like buildings, or for that matter anything else that man makes to serve a purpose, must be designed.

Art, believes Whitaker, must have a purpose beyond the outlet of the artist's emotional fervor. Design, or its lack, makes the difference between an esthetic painting and one that merely reports. All masterpieces in art exhibit sound design, whether the intention is abstract or representational.

Good abstract examples represent pure design which, considered as ends in themselves, can be both beautiful and inspiring. As a long time designer of ecclesiastical art, Whitaker knows the importance of such pure, non-communicative design. However, he feels strongly that design alone does not make a picture, since its presence cannot convey a meaning to the viewer. Because Whitaker desires to communicate through the vehicle of his painting, he believes in the validity of a "realistic" expression—one in which, in addition to its abstract foundation, will contain the humanly edifying content of atmosphere, depth, and pictorial identity.

192 Doris White

Doris White

Silent City
Watercolor 23" x 36"
Collection, Mr. and Mrs. John Proctor

Doris White continually tries to exploit all the possibilities of watercolor by working on either a slick or rough surface, painting wet-in-wet with soft, subtle areas blending together, or with crisp, sharp edges here and there. This experimentation increases a sensitivity to what the paint can or cannot do.

The artist does not paint from nature directly, nor does she draw on the paper beforehand. The idea grows and changes as it evolves. This approach permits her complete freedom to change directions, re-evaluate, and reject. Sometimes, when a visual image emerges, she may abandon her direction altogether, letting an intense area of color give way to a series of somber hues, subtle in value.

Doris White prefers completing one watercolor before starting another. This may involve several hours on one painting, or several days, but she carries it through while still stimulated and motivated by an idea. She finds that watercolor can be worked on as slowly and deliberately as oil. With a sponge and clean water, an area can be kept moist and, if necessary, *lifted* to expose the white of the paper.

In watercolor, she experiments with a variety of surfaces, using only paper of the highest quality. This same regard is also applied to colors that are permanent. Because of the wide range available to the artist, she does not adhere to a limited palette. The colors she selects are determined by the ultimate effect desired. She works primarily in terms of warm and cool colors. Here again, experimenting with the intermixing of paints is vital to becoming familiar with all the possibilities of the colors at her command. She uses them first with a wash brush filled with water and then, for contrast, she adds strokes of dry brush. Doris White is constantly aware of the transparency of each color she mixes. Earth colors—such as ochre and burnt sienna—tend to be opaque when used alone or in combination with transparent paints. Rich grays may be obtained by intermixing these opaques with transparent colors, such as phthalocyanine blue and green, or alizarin crimson.

Besides the usual small round to wide flat wash brushes, the artist has used sticks, bamboo, brush handles, irregular pieces of wood, and knives and razor blades to scrape away areas of paint. Blotters, sponges, and paper toweling are used on occasion for redistributing wash areas, and controlling shapes when working wet-in-wet. She finds a flat, metal palette—such as a white enamel butchers' tray—useful for mixing large amounts of color. She does not restrict herself to conventional materials, since she feels that many handy objects may be potential tools for the artist.

194   Edgar A. Whitney

Abandoned
Watercolor 14¾" x 21½"
Collection, Robert E. Conlan

Edgar whitney believes that anything but 100% all-rag paper makes a tough job even tougher. He finds that a 140 lb is a good all-around weight—heavy enough to permit corrections—and it can be used on the other side if necessary. Whitney does not mount his paper, because an occasional bulge in his sheet does not warrant the time and effort required for mounting. He clips his 140 lb paper to a piece of Masonite, one strong clip at each corner. A bulge can be pressed out and the clips readjusted in a second. When he uses a pencil, a 2B makes a mark dark enough to be seen under a wash without furrowing the paper. He frequently draws directly with a goose quill, with a ballpoint pen, or with a brush.

Whitney does most of his painting with a 2″ camel's hair flat brush and a 1″ red sable flat. In many pictures, no other brushes are used at all. This may be because demonstrating to classes everyday, and talking while he paints, he finds these brushes faster. However, he does prefer to have available the best tool for every solution. Therefore, he also has a no. 4 rigger; nos. 2, 3, 6, 10, 14 red sable round brushes; and a 1″ red sable flat. He also uses what he calls a "Whitney Rotary," a double-ended brush, which enables him to paint with water in one brush and color in the other. With this brush, an edge can be treated or softened instantly by a flip of the hand to the water-filled brush, then back to the color-filled brush. To construct the double-ended brush, he joins the two brushes where the diameters are equal—a wedge cut into one handle and a *V* that fits into the wedge in the other—which he binds with fine thread, a little Duco cement, and then covers with waterproof adhesive.

Whitney uses an O'Hara palette, upon which the color is a mound on a flat surface. The reason for this is that sullied colors run off and leave pure color available on the top of the mound. A dinner plate or enameled tray has the same advantage. Arranging the colors from warm to cold, Whitney uses vermilion, cadmium orange, cadmium yellow deep, strontium yellow, viridian, phthalocyanine green, Prussian blue, cobalt blue, ultramarine blue, alizarin crimson. Those are his brights, kept at the top of his slightly tilted palette, so that the sullied color does not run into them. In the lower row, he has Indian red, burnt sienna, yellow ochre, raw umber, burnt umber, Payne's gray, and ivory black. All these colors are reasonably permanent and he can obtain any desired tint or shade.

In addition to this standard equipment, Whitney also keeps miscellaneous items on hand for specific tasks: a large synthetic sponge adjacent to his palette helps him maintain a precise degree of wetness in his brushes; a rubber sink scraper for stroking in finely lit planes on rocks; a rubber heel, cut at different angles to set in smaller rocks; Kleenex to pick out colors; a toothbrush for color spatter; and sandpaper for textural effects, are among the items he has used.

Frank Wilcox (1887–1964) usually painted with transparent watercolor, since it seemed to afford the readiest interpretation of the fleeting effects of light during the day and the season. However, even when employing opaque media, he always tried to combine it with transparent passages so that architecture and figures were tied in with a freely treated landscape. Starting a composition depended much upon this thought, and, in watercolor, he controlled this effect by predetermined transitional tones used either as an under- or over-glaze. Generally, the tonal contrast between sky and skyline determined the tone of the work; while the shadow depths in each plane deepened and became warmer as he worked forward in the picture plane. When this key was set, Wilcox was able to estimate the tone of partially detached areas surrounded by uncovered paper. He respected the transparency or opacity of paints, their ductility, carrying force, and solubility when such colors were found adjacent or over-glazed.

For Wilcox, one of the best ways to produce the effect of sharp sunlight in the foregrounds was to overlap lighted surfaces with shadow tones. This is a variation of the usual procedure, but it develops keen edges and an automatic illusion of reflected light within such shadows.

Wilcox did most of his work on rough, mounted paper, 22" x 30". As a rule, he used only three brushes: one large flat brush and round and pointed sables. He used a common kitchen chair as an easel, preferring the simplest equipment.

When working in the Ohio landscape, where Wilcox lived, he used the following palette: yellow ochre, cadmium yellow pale, cobalt blue, ultramarine, viridian, rose madder, light red, burnt sienna, and Payne's gray. Elsewhere, he discovered additions to this palette were necessary: reds and yellows for the far West, and additional blues and cadmium red when he painted in maritime Quebec.

Towards the end of his life and while invalided from a long illness, the artist frequently drew on bond paper, often directly with a felt pen and watercolor washes added. In the painting on the facing page, Wilcox demonstrates his characteristic techniques. Every line, dot, and mass contributed to an over-all impression. The artist used a felt tip pen in a dry-brush manner to integrate it with the color wash. Many of these little watercolors represent a kind of artistic nostalgia, a return to the romantic scene of his youth when rural America was colored by a quieter way of life, to the times and places that left indelible impressions on his memory. He left a collection of over four hundred of these brilliant sketches.

Loran Wilford

Clowns Resting
Watercolor 11" x 15"

ACCORDING TO LORAN WILFORD, all the brilliant technique in the world will not suffice if the artist does not have something to say that is significant. Technique alone is never enough, whether the method is abstraction, expressionism, or realism. When one departs too far from the fundamental idea of life or nature, the result is merely a performance.

Technique, then, is for Wilford merely a means to an end. His own pictorial ideas are based on the familiar around him, his inspiration is drawn from the things he has seen and remembered. Sometimes a few lines on paper in pen or pencil, perhaps a small watercolor sketch made on the spot will suffice as the basis for an ambitious composition. More often than not, it is just a memory of something out of the past. He tries to be himself as nearly as he can be in his painting: to paint as well as he knows how; to feel his subject as profoundly as possible by trying to interpret his way of life.

Wilford likes any good watercolor paper (from 70 to 400 lb) that will take a wash, and he chooses the paper for each painting that will help him to express his ideas. Sometimes a wet manner is right; sometimes a dry one.

His brushes are nos. 9, 10, and 12 round sables, plus a 1" and a 2½" house-painter's brush for the big lay-ins. He uses a knife for scraping, and sometimes a sponge or the palms of his hand to gain certain desired textures.

The watercolor reproduced here was developed entirely from sketches in ink. (He frequently makes such drawings with a felt tipped pen; he modifies the shapes of the pen ends to achieve some of those effects that may seem impossible with the standard nibs.) Wilford still paints on-the-spot quite a bit, but sometimes things happen so quickly that a few lines are all that can be put down. In the actual painting of the scene, much depends on memory. Perhaps this is just as well, he feels for then one retains only the essence of the form and color.

SANTA ANA, NEW MEXICO

Santa Ana, New Mexico, 1965
Watercolor 21½" x 29"
Collection, Mr. and Mrs. C. C. Beall

LUMEN WINTER'S APPROACH to watercolor painting is unorthodox. His first attempts were made at the age of three with a cheap box of colors and a small camel's hair brush, on plain white paper. Since that time, he has used everything from brown paper and gouache to the most expensive rag papers and the finest colors available. Recently, he has taken care to select materials which are lasting: colors which will retain their brilliance, and paper which has been manufactured without the use of acids.

The artist selects his paper on the basis of the specific painting he intends to do: rough papers for broad, free-wheeling statements; and smooth paper when a subject requires careful rendering of detail. His selection of brushes also depends on the painting itself. He believes one can paint with anything from a good housepainting brush to the finest red sable. The choice depends on the concept one wishes to record.

His palette is simple: yellow ochre, raw sienna, cadmium yellow, light cobalt blue, ultramarine blue, cerulean blue, Payne's gray, burnt umber, vermilion, alizarin crimson, permanent green, and viridian green—colors which he feels will supply just about any hue or tone he desires. He considers blotters, sponges, various textured cloths, and other devices for scratching out the dried paper to be legitimate tools for the watercolorist.

The watercolor reproduced here—painted in a demonstration before guests of the American Watercolor Society—was completed in fifteen minutes. First, he prepared two large containers of water—one for use in color, and one for rinsing brushes. The upper portion of the painting was done on wet paper in a heavy wash of Payne's gray, cobalt, and ultramarine blue, with a small amount of burnt umber. For the sky, he used a good quality 2" boar's hair housepainting brush; the lower area of the painting was rendered—on dry paper—with a no. 6 pointed sable and ½" round Japanese brush.

James Couper Wright

Still Life with Melons
Watercolor 23" x 29"
Collection, Mr. and Mrs. James E. Nelson

When JAMES COUPER WRIGHT does a watercolor, he works almost flat on an adjustable drawing table. The subject matter determines the weight and surface of the paper, whether it will be rough textured or smooth. He soaks the paper, then presses it to the surface of the table. Ninety percent of the time, he uses a no. 1 or a no. 2 flat sable brush. He keeps the paper wet by working over all the areas. Using a palette which contains more than a dozen colors, Wright starts with the light tones, then goes to the middle and dark tones. He begins with almost abstract rectangular shapes which he later cuts into with darks. He keeps the whole thing fairly wet.

Wright likes to work on a large sheet, sometimes as big as 26" x 40". The technique used in a painting depends, for him, on the character of the subject matter and it is all thought out ahead of time, even to the timing. Then even the happy accidents can be incorporated into the painting. He keeps designing with his strokes, always pulling them up.

Wright usually makes many detail sketches which he may later use in a painting. Sometimes he starts to paint color patterns, combinations of things he remembers. He finds a felt pen good for figure sketches. It has its limitations, but it moves quickly for his purposes. He always does his painting *indoors*, sometimes from memory, an ability in which he has trained himself. He almost never paints what he sees, even if he works from an actual set-up.

In *Still Life with Melons*, reproduced here, he worked from imagination, since he had been working with melons and fruits with his students. "From the impact of all this sensuous beauty," Wright said, "I visualized a very vibrant still life. The only way to paint this *feeling* is to do so by starting with a *bang*; to continue and finish with a bang!"

Lacks distinctiveness

ANDREW WYETH HAS A VERY POSITIVE feeling about watercolor. He understands that one cannot exactly carry out a predetermined effect in a fluid technique. Chance enters into it no matter how skillful and experienced the artist may be. The paper must be precisely the right degree of dampness here, dryness there; the brush must be loaded properly; and a false stroke in a vital spot is irreparable. Wyeth does not sponge out or labor over weak passages; either it comes off the first try, or he casts aside the paper and makes a fresh start. Wyeth seldom spends longer than a half hour on a watercolor. But weeks may have preceded the study and the building up of the mood of that watercolor.

Many of Wyeth's pictures are painted on location, but he also does them in his studio after considerable study of the subject in nature. Frequently he makes a rapid sketch on the spot in pencil or pen and, with this note, develops his watercolor in the studio.

Wyeth works on a medium rough watercolor paper which he has made up in 22" x 30" blocks. He objects to stretched paper because he believes it loses its capacity for brilliant effects. He does all his painting with three sable brushes, nos. 5, 10, and 15, without ever using broad flat brushes for covering large washes. In view of the gusto with which Wyeth works, one is astonished to see such a small palette in his hand, especially since in his rapid painting he requires a quantity of "runny" washes on short order.

In beginning a watercolor, Wyeth lays in the large masses in their approximate colors very rapidly, but without detail definition. This may or may not have been preceded by a slight pencil indication. Thus, the paper is entirely covered in the first few moments, except for white areas which are untouched by the brush. Wyeth never uses white body color. Occasionally white, or near-white is obtained by a heavy stroke of the brush handle in a still-wet wash. Working back into the wet areas, he develops his picture, pulling definition out of the blurred color masses, working all over the picture while it is still moist.

In his temperas, in contrast to his watercolors, Wyeth's objective is to cover up his brush strokes and to obtain a sense of freedom through pattern rather than technique. He paints his temperas with a single sable brush not over ¾" long, on Masonite upon which three coats of whiting mixed with casein glue are applied as a ground. The pulverized glue is heated, in water, in a double boiler. Wyeth sandpapers the final coat to a very smooth finish. The panel is made rigid by a framework attached to the back. He paints with dry colors mixed with distilled water and egg yolk on his palette as he works.

In his tempera painting, Wyeth's procedure is to make a monochrome underpainting in black ink. The colors, applied over this black and white, have a quality of weight and depth which he prefers to direct painting in color.

206   Nat Youngblood

Nᴇᴀʀʟʏ ᴀʟʟ ᴏꜰ ɴᴀᴛ ʏᴏᴜɴɢʙʟᴏᴏᴅ's ᴘᴀɪɴᴛɪɴɢs are produced for the color pages of *The Pittsburgh Press* Sunday magazine. He works both by assignment from the editor and on his own inspiration, depending on what seems best at a particular time.

Because he is constantly on the go, his equipment is compact: an easel unit which has a drawer for brushes, paints, and palette, and folds into a small, light case with a handle. He can carry this in one hand and a jar of water and paper in the other; a notebook in his hip pocket; and a camera over his shoulder.

Youngblood finds a rough watercolor board most practical and always carries a half dozen 15" x 20" sheets. Its stiff backing eliminates the need for a drawing board. His largest brush is a no. 20 round sable; flats and rounds of various sizes in sable, and one large flat bristle brush complete the list. Some brushes are frazzled and worn into a variety of odd shapes, but serve him well for certain effects. Small brushes are replaced often. If the subject is complicated, he uses soft charcoal, kneaded eraser, and carbon pencils for preliminary structure drawings.

In the field, Youngblood carries a limited palette—alizarin crimson, spectrum red, burnt sienna, cadmium lemon, ultramarine, Prussian blue, and lamp black. These are for pure watercolor painting, but occasionally he uses tube tempera and/or casein.

If Youngblood has any single characteristic approach to his painting, it would be lack of routine. Traveling light, working under a climate of emergency, he has been forced to assume an expedient and adjustable attitude. His paintings are often done directly, and at times have gone straight to the color engraver. Usually, however, he reworks and finishes them in his home studio. Sometimes he rolls the paint on heavy and wet, depending on the local value and color. In another instance, he may prefer a dry application, in a subject of pure light and mood. Sometimes he turns the paper in all directions, holding it high and low, directing the wet color to desired areas. He often uses a pen to define certain details.

His procedure is generally as follows: after deciding on a subject and his feelings about it, he does preliminary doodles in pencil or even in color, in order to "spot" dark areas and linear design and to test ideas that occur. Next, light charcoal structure lines are applied. Picking up the brush, he continues further with light, broad color suggestions, still searching for structure. If passages of brilliant transparent color are to show, they are applied at this point. Now medium darks are added to "freeze" the design and general composition. From this point on, he works back and forth in values and color. Toward the end, Youngblood uses thin black lines or opaque color for final definition.

William Zorach

Bay Point, Maine
Watercolor 15" x 22"

William zorach (1887–1966) used only traditional equipment—no unusual paints or exotic devices for peculiar effects. Like many straight-forward painters, he depended upon the classic palette: lemon yellow, cadmium yellow pale, cadmium yellow orange, vermilion, rose madder, cobalt, cerulean, French ultramarine, burnt sienna, raw umber, Winsor green, viridian, and ivory black. He preferred hot pressed, lightweight paper, never heavier than 120 lb, cutting a full sheet in half so that his pictures are approximately 15" x 22".

Starting with a sketchy charcoal outline, Zorach followed with a cold water washdown of the entire sheet with a moist sponge. Most of the drawing was thus removed, except for a faint line visible enough to reveal the main structure of his composition. Favoring those qualities resulting from a wet surface, he made certain to maintain uniform dampness (never soaking) and during the entire process of painting retained these qualities by repeated sponges on the back of the paper.

Next follows a general tone, laid over the whole sheet before getting down to the main problem. This is a device that immediately establishes a harmonious background for the color to follow, and also eliminates the frequently objectionable harshness of a pure-white surface. Such a ground provides a shortcut to quick results; while still wet, lighter areas may be picked out with the aid of blotters or paper tissues. From then on, it is a matter of proceeding with the usual manner until the painting is completed.

Zorach seldom touched a picture once he was back home; all work was usually completed at the spot. (Incidentally, he preferred early morning or late afternoon for his sessions with watercolor; he did not like midday for painting, claiming "the light is all wrong!")

Zorach objected to the use of opaque paint in any form, either when it is used blatantly so that all may know, or even used surreptitiously in minute doses. Like many loyal worshippers of watercolor, he preferred the distinctive translucency which is the earmark of the medium, rejecting any interloper that would endanger its existence.

I wouldn't have the ptg?

Milford Zornes

Beach Party
Watercolor   20½" x 28½"
Collection, William Colville, Jr.

In the practice of painting watercolors, Milford Zornes keeps equipment, technical devices, and theoretical concepts of design and structure to a simplified minimum. His palette is based upon the fundamental premise that, of all the possible means of achieving contrast and relationships with color, the differentiation between warm and cool color is the most important to the painter. Therefore, Zornes maintains that the basic concept of the palette is more or less complete if it contains the warm and cool elements, whether it be composed of one color in each category or a dozen of each, plus black.

Zornes differs with those who argue that black should be left off the palette, but he feels it must be used with care and should be considered as a color and as a means of making neutral shades when they are needed. Black must not be allowed to lure one to depend upon value contrasts where contrasts of color intensities would be more exciting and desirable.

The artist experiments a great deal within the principle of the warm and cool aspects of color, choosing the most transparent colors, since the very nature of the medium dictates this quality. At times he finds Naples yellow useful, even though it is a somewhat opaque color. He seldom uses white. His working palette for on-the-spot painting consists of about sixteen colors, divided between warm and cool, and arranged on a wide plastic palette which he holds in his left hand as he would an oil palette.

He uses four or five brushes, ranging from a fine-pointed, long-haired Japanese brush to a 2" wide flat ox hair—with a 1" flat sable wash brush and a no. 16 round ox hair being the two most used.

Zornes has deliberately made a technique of painting outdoors on imperial size sheets (approximately 22" x 30"), always striving to bring to these papers the same spontaneity and breadth that is more typically realized on smaller sizes. He uses top quality paper, such as a 300 lb French paper, rough or smooth, and and an English 400 lb sheet. These papers do not require stretching and will stand a great deal of handling in folios and in and out of frames. In addition, he fills scores of sketchbooks with small, quick watercolors and drawings.

I like the locale, peoples, color
community etc